5 STEPS TO PROFESSIONAL PRESENCE

5 STEPS TO PROFESSIONAL PRESENCE

How to Project Confidence,
Competence, and Credibility at Work

Susan Bixler and Lisa Scherrer Dugan

Adams Media Corporation
Holbrook, Massachusetts

Published by
Adams Media Corporation
260 Center Street, Holbrook, MA 02343
www.adamsmedia.com

ISBN: 1-58062-442-1

Printed in United States of America.

J I H G F E D C B A

Library of Congress Cataloging-in-Publication Data
available from the publisher.

This publication is designed to provide accurate and authoritative information with regard to the subject matter covered. It is sold with the understanding that the publisher is not engaged in rendering legal, accounting, or
other professional advice. If legal advice or other expert assistance is required,
the services of a competent professional person should be sought.
—From a *Declaration of Principles* jointly adopted by a Committee of the
American Bar Association and a Committee of Publishers and Associations

This book is available at quantity discounts for bulk purchases.
For information, call 1-800-872-5627.

Visit our exciting small business Web site: www.businesstown.com

To Chris and Kyle

Our encouragement, our life, our kids

Contents

Step One
Recognize the Inherent Power
of Your Professional Presence / 1

Step Two
Establish Effective Nonverbal Communication / 53

Step Three
Create Your Virtual Presence / 91

Step Four
Understand Business Etiquette / 125

Step Five
Develop Social Savvy / 195

Acknowledgments

Some of our clients and friends couldn't believe that we were going back to them again for more quotes and all the corporate war stories they would share with us. "Didn't you ask for my opinion on that in 1985?" they wanted to know. Five books in twenty years makes us more grateful than ever for those friends and clients who continue to share their perspective. While some of the questions may remain the same, the answers only get better.

It's not the Academy Awards, but we still have a lot of people in our lives to thank. We would like to extend our special thanks and gratitude to Lynn Seligman, the best of literary agents, and Ed Walters, the best of editors. Then there are our clients, friends, and family. Tim, Mama B, Joey Bixler–Clifton, Larissa Bixler, Mike, Tracy Penticuff, Alicia Edwards, Kerry Kerr, David Deans, Lee Kricher, Lisa Steiner, Page Haviland, Jerry Dankel, Ann Herrmann, Pat Herrmann, Jim Fuqua, Darlene Caplan, Dave Zarzour, Claire Bowen, Mary Yates, Sterling Nelson, Lynne Henderson, Margarita Porto, Pam Grundon, Pauline Brandt, Skip Kinford, Bill Delmont, Teresa Owens Unser, Kevin Patton, Juliana Deans, and Dana Kuebler . . . we'll be back for more of your wisdom, insights, and experience.

Introduction

We live in a world where the velocity of change is a given. We have no choice—we have to build our business relationships rapidly or we get lost in the dust.

Technology has given us more ways to do this than ever before—e-mail, voice mail, and e-commerce for starters. There is, however, a basic human need to see and interact with other people. Our brain responds 60,000 times faster to the stimuli of face-to-face human contact than with non-face-to-face contact.

Five Steps to Professional Presence includes one step on virtual presence, but four steps that deal with our face-to-face human interaction. While technology in business has had a very productive impact in our lives, strengths can be overused. Too much technology can and has depersonalized many of our relationships.

Sophocles in 500 B.C.E. wrote, "Nothing vast enters the life of mortals without a curse." The impact of the Internet can only be described as vast beyond anything we have ever seen. But it doesn't negate our need as humans to interact with each other in person.

Again looking to the past for wisdom, a wonderful book, *Manners, Culture and Dress* published in 1890 shows how little has changed around human contact. While the words are more formal, the inherent message is the same. A sense of continuity bridges today's high-tech world with the business environment of over 100 years ago. We have selected a quote from this book to begin each of the 17 chapters. In most cases, the quote summarizes the ensuing chapter almost perfectly.

The foundations of human interaction haven't changed all that much over the centuries, but the peripheral environment has. *Five Steps to Professional Presence* provides valuable skills that you can use to increase your effectiveness with people, present yourself professionally both electronically and in-person, self promote with credibility, manage meetings with competence, and handle social situations with savvy.

Most business books never get read beyond Chapter 1. So to address this, we have designed *Five Steps* so that you can go straight to the table of contents, determine the step that will provide you with the most immediate benefit, and turn to that part of the book.

> We shall not cease from exploration and the end of all our exploring will be to arrive where we started, and know the place for the first time.
> —T.S. Eliot

Of course, ultimately we feel that no matter where you start, you will benefit by reading the entire book, because chances are you will find stories and examples that will hit home.

We thank you for purchasing this book. Maybe, one hundred years from now, it will get dusted off and used as a reference by another author for a business etiquette book in the year 2101. While the human aspect will probably remain much the same, the technology will, of course, be profoundly different.

The end game, the deliverable of this book is to help you become more successful, whether this means making more money, being happier at work, or positioning yourself for greater management and leadership responsibilities.

What Is Your PPQ (Professional Presence Quotient)?

One of the ways we like to measure the knowledge that seminar participants have gained during one of our sessions is to test them by using true or false questions before and after the seminar. They are usually amazed at how many professional presence questions they simply cannot answer.

By testing your base of information before you read this book, you will have concrete proof by the end of the book of how much you have learned from *Five Steps to Professional Presence*. After taking the PPQ quiz, check your responses against the answers at the end of the test.

T F

❏ ❏ 1. A firm handshake is only offered to a businessman, not a business-woman.

❏ ❏ 2. Changing a meeting location can often change the attitude of the meeting.

❏ ❏ 3. Socially, a man should wait for a woman in business to offer her hand.

❏ ❏ 4. The person you most want to honor is always mentioned first in an introduction. Gender is not a consideration.

❏ ❏ 5. Exchange business cards at the beginning of the meeting.

❏ ❏ 6. Every industry has its own wardrobe requirements. One standard is not appropriate for everyone.

❏ ❏ 7. A decisive statement can be negated by weak body language.

❏ ❏ 8. It is easier to influence others in person than over the phone or by letter.

❏ ❏ 9. The best way to handle a chit-chatter is to stand up and walk toward the door.

T F

❑ ❑ 10. Heaving your shoulders and shooting a cryptic look can be a stronger message than your verbal one.

❑ ❑ 11. If someone repeats a sentence several times while looking at the floor, swallowing hard, and putting a hand in front of the mouth, he or she is probably lying.

❑ ❑ 12. The use of silence is a powerful way to establish presence.

❑ ❑ 13. Taking notes at a meeting is rather rude because you must break eye contact to do it.

❑ ❑ 14. The most effective meetings are no more than 30 minutes.

❑ ❑ 15. Don't provide an agenda unless it is a large, full-day meeting.

❑ ❑ 16. Recapping information for latecomers is a considerate thing to do.

❑ ❑ 17. At a meeting, make eye contact with each person until you have determined the color of his or her eyes.

❑ ❑ 18. The power perch is the seat to the right of the head of the table.

❑ ❑ 19. Sit as close to the leader as protocol permits.

❑ ❑ 20. The office grapevine is 50 percent accurate.

❑ ❑ 21. Less than 1 percent of the population can keep a secret.

❑ ❑ 22. Keeping up with a client's sport or family interest is a form of courtesy.

❑ ❑ 23. Businesspeople who are current on news events are generally considered current on business issues, too.

❑ ❑ 24. It is impossible to be considered sophisticated without a working knowledge of manners.

❑ ❑ 25. If a joke is not funny, but not offensive, laugh anyway.

❑ ❑ 26. The only time to privately call attention to someone's appearance or behavior mistake is when he or she can do something about it.

❑ ❑ 27. Staying calm and apologizing is particularly important when you have made a severe faux pas.

❑ ❑ 28. Reacting to someone's embarrassment by trying to share in the blame or relating to it as something you have done in the past is a gracious gesture.

❑ ❑ 29. E-mail is one of the best methods to communicate subtle, complex, or personalized information.

T F

❑ ❑ 30. Sending a carefully constructed, well-thought-out e-mail containing information that will contribute to a colleague's project demonstrates presence.

❑ ❑ 31. Cell phones are an exceptional business tool that can be used in any environment to move business or personal issues forward.

❑ ❑ 32. Voice mail is a mechanical method of transmitting information and will cause you to lose presence. Faxing a letter is better.

❑ ❑ 33. Cartoon transmittal sheets lighten up any message and are especially good for negative information.

❑ ❑ 34. Standing up while on the phone will increase the quality of your voice.

❑ ❑ 35. Ask to get on a client's appointment calendar with an important phone call the same way you would an in-person appointment.

❑ ❑ 36. Return all phone calls the same day, even if it is in the evening.

❑ ❑ 37. Eating a one-course meal before a business event is considered smart if you have a large appetite.

❑ ❑ 38. Don't order anything that can't be eaten attractively, like corn on the cob, juicy hamburgers, large sandwiches, and long pasta noodles with tomato sauce.

❑ ❑ 39. When invited to play sports with a client, be honest about your playing ability.

❑ ❑ 40. Community involvement is part of creating professional presence.

8. True	16. False	24. True	32. False	40. True
7. True	15. False	23. True	31. False	39. True
6. True	14. True	22. True	30. True	38. True
5. True	13. False	21. True	29. False	37. True
4. True	12. True	20. False	28. True	36. True
3. True	11. True	19. True	27. True	35. True
2. True	10. True	18. True	26. True	34. True
1. False	9. True	17. True	25. True	33. False

Answers

- ✐ *If your total score was 35 correct or higher,* you have a great deal of professional presence knowledge and will be able to use this book to affirm many of the things you are already doing correctly and fine-tune others.
- ✐ *If your total score was 30 to 34 correct,* you know many of the basics, but this book will help fill in the more sophisticated or complex issues inherent in image.
- ✐ *If your total score was less than 30,* this book will provide you with all the basics plus an understanding of more advanced skills.

In all cases, after you have read *Five Steps to Professional Presence*, please go back and retake the PPQ quiz. We can promise an increased awareness and probably a perfect score!

Five Steps to Professional Presence is a composite of our book *Professional Presence*, published in 1991, and the latest in business practices. It is the synthesis of our personal perspective as well as that of our clients. We have met with businesspeople, both on an individual and group basis, to discuss presence and how it is interpreted in their industry. *Five Steps to Professional Presence* is the coming together of 20 years of information presented at our seminars and hundreds of years of experience of experts before our time. This book will give you the skills necessary to showcase your abilities. Your personal power and presence will become formidable, recognized, and appreciated in as you create your own unique competitive advantage!

Step One

Recognize the Inherent Power of Your Professional Presence

Make First Impressions
Lasting Impressions

The bow is the proper mode of salutation to exchange between acquaintances in public, and, in certain circumstances in private. The bow should never be a mere nod. A gentleman should raise his hat completely from his head and slightly incline the whole body.

—*Manners, Culture and Dress, 1890*

At the first company picnic she attended, Linda was determined to initiate conversation and make good first impressions. Her three-word mantra was "friendly, gracious, and confident." She spotted her boss and asked him to introduce her to the new CEO standing beside him. Suddenly, Nick, a regional manager with a reputation for unwanted kisses, hugs, and verbal jabs, intercepted her, waving his cigar. He shouted, "Hey, Linda, I heard you just lost the Melrose account. A six-footer like you should sit down more. Those guys at Melrose are midgets. Ha. Ha."

We have all been in situations like this. Usually afterward, we can think of several dozen brilliant retorts. But at that moment, Linda's mind was blank. Still, Nick was

> According to a study done by the University of Connecticut, first impressions turn out to be 67 percent accurate.

one of those people who is hard to ignore. It also seemed that everyone was looking at Linda, waiting to see what she would do.

She didn't wait for Nick to grab her, slap her on the back, and further assault her with his typical, "How's your love life?" She walked up to him, gave him a token smile, offered a limp handshake, and a few brief words but with direct, unwavering eye contact. Then she moved purposefully toward her boss and the new CEO, working hard to be "friendly, gracious, and confident."

Does she normally offer a forced smile and a fishlike clasp? No. But in the context of the situation, it was the best option.

First impressions can be effective or disastrous, but they are usually lasting. Our objective in meeting others is to establish comfort, trust, and rapport, and it's not always easy—even without unwanted interference.

Some people intentionally create orchestrated power plays to make others feel intimidated. One buyer from a large department store refused to make eye contact with anyone in sales. When salespeople would walk through her door, she kept her eyes riveted to whatever information was on her desk at the time. She would verbally greet everyone and even answer questions, but she never looked up. The salespeople felt that they were no more important to her than an annoying fly in her office.

Really savvy salespeople would just sit there and not speak. Although their hearts were pounding because she often controlled 40 percent of their quota, they refused to talk to the top of her head. Until they felt they were receiving the respect they deserved, they just clammed up and waited for eye contact.

> An executive in a large corporation stated, "I allow three to four minutes for a salesperson to establish credibility. The three-part criterion is simple: appearance, communication skills, and the value of the service. If the appearance and the communication skills are poor, the sale is already lost because I stop listening."

Buck and His Mooseheads

Another difficulty is to be acknowledged briefly and then ignored and dismissed. Another client of ours experienced orchestrated intimidation at its best on her first visit with the manager of a manufacturing firm. His secretary showed her in, and there sat Buck, leaning back in his chair, black alligator shoes braced against the front of his desk, phone propped against his shoulder. He nodded in brief greeting, and while she waited for him to finish his conversation, she looked around at the mooseheads and other trophies on the wall and the photographs of Buck at the helm of racing speedboats.

When he finished the call, he stayed seated and reached out to shake hands. For her, it was an awkward stretch.

For 10 minutes his phone continued to ring and he answered it. His shoes stayed on the mahogany desk and the speedboats continued racing around the office. She felt out-manned, out-gunned, and she knew it. She realized that if she stayed much longer, she would lose not only the sale but her faltering self-esteem. So she suggested, "Buck, let's go down to the company cafeteria for coffee."

Not only was Buck unable to transport his speedboats and deceased animal heads to the cafeteria, he also had to keep his feet on the floor. Away from his home turf and telephone, she was able to re-establish herself and make her presentation. After a bad start and a weak first impression, the only course was to change the location and start over.

Although she didn't sell him anything at that meeting, she followed up for three months, and eventually introduced an entire communication program to the company.

After the implementation of the program, Buck and she talked about that first meeting. "You know, Lynne," he said, "when you moved us out of that office of mine, that's when I figured you might be able to help our staff. They are tough and combative. I tell them they are like cats marching in a parade—everybody doing their own thing and resisting input or advice. So after our first meeting, where I really worked to intimidate you, I was impressed enough with how you handled yourself to continue to evaluate your program."

Buck continued, "In fact, in my old office, I used to sit in an antique barber chair that kept me towering three feet above everyone else. I intimidated at least eighty percent of the people that walked through my door, but I figured that the other twenty percent were the only people that I wanted to do business with anyway!"

So it is possible to overcome intimidation and a difficult beginning. Changing the meeting location is one method. But staying

A well-known author on a national book tour spoke to a large group of businesspeople in Chicago. His book dealt with personal character development and the years and experiences that it takes to build it. A rather mild-mannered admirer was sitting in the front row of the session, quietly taking pictures with his digital camera as the author began his remarks. The author noticed him immediately and flew into a rage. "I am not available to you!" he shouted. His microphone amplified his words throughout the room. "Who are those pictures for? You are impolite. You are rude. Don't you understand that I am not available to you!!" The room of 400 people became so quiet that crumbling a tissue would have made a racket. The offending amateur photographer offered his sincere apologies and put away his camera. The audience was left thinking what an unforgettable and lasting first impression this author had made and wondering how many more experiences would be required of him before he had built the character that his book addressed.

unruffled because you know how to calmly and confidently manage your presence is the most powerful.

Overcoming intentional intimidation is just one hurdle to conquer in making a powerful first impression. Where to sit in a meeting, what to do in the reception area, how to execute impressive physical contact, when to give out business cards, how to make introductions, synchronize your body language, and appear warm and friendly without flirting are the central issues to making an impact.

First, let's look at some forms of physical contact that can create a confusing message.

A Kiss Is Just a Kiss . . . Or Is It?

A colleague told us of a manager that would kiss every female he was introduced to. A businesswoman would extend her hand for a handshake and Harold would take it, reach for her shoulders with his other hand, and head straight for a smooch and an embrace.

To those who watched Harold in action, two things became obvious. First, rarely was anyone flattered. Nearly everyone was embarrassed, suspicious, or insulted. Secondly, women who had met Harold before quickly learned to avoid his kisses. They developed the stiff-elbow, step-back counterattack to elude the unwanted embrace and inappropriate kiss.

Harold thought his technique was smooth and that his affectionate approach was the best way to endear himself to new female business acquaintances. He viewed it as his personal trademark. He never realized what was happening—that he was clearly building a barrier between himself and his female customers.

Greeting new business acquaintances in the United States with a kiss is a mistake. Although it may be expected in France and other parts of the world, it is usually out of place on Wall Street or Main Street USA.

In the United States, when you kiss a new business associate, you are pretending that you immediately share a close relationship. It fools no one and usually creates discomfort, which is exactly the opposite of what you want to accomplish.

> In most cases, it is the woman who decides if a handshake will turn into a kiss.

There are several exceptions. If your corporate culture or your industry encourages hugs and friendly embraces, then join in if it is part of your own style. If not, don't be coerced into doing it. The second exception is when you are greeting a longtime business colleague whom you haven't seen for quite a while. A kiss that doesn't leave lipstick marks (if you leave your mark, quickly and casually rub it off) and a big hug will show genuine warmth.

In most cases, it is the woman who decides if a handshake will turn into a kiss.

Hey, Look Me Over

Whenever we walk into a room, our clothing, manners, and mannerisms are on display. Others assess our self-confidence and our ability to present ourselves based on 60 seconds of information. Each of us has our own signature of professional presence—an indelible statement that we make the instant we show up. It is the energy we bring into a room, along with the confidence and initiative we demonstrate. It affords us an opportunity to connect immediately.

That's why we recommend the 30-second Detail Check for maximum impact. Think of it as a professional presence checklist. No pilot takes off without doing a visual check of the plane to make sure everything is A-OK. No scuba diver jumps off a boat without making sure the air valves are working. And no businessperson should walk into a meeting without the detail check.

The 30-second Detail Check before a meeting gives you the reassurance to concentrate on people and the discussion. You don't need to wonder about broken zippers, lunch remnants on your tie, or runs in your hosiery.

Find a restroom and start at the top. Whether you are wearing business casual or traditional business dress, the 30-second Detail Check is necessary. Check your hair, remembering that you are seen more from the back than from the front. Check to see that nothing is stuck between your teeth. Check your nose, especially if you have a cold or sinus trouble. Check for dandruff, stains, and open buttons. Women need to be sure that there is no lipstick on their teeth and that makeup is well blended. If you are wearing dressy business casual or traditional attire and are headed for a meeting, put your jacket on. It adds to your presence. Remember that we are seen more from the waist up because we spend much more time seated.

> A new salesperson inadvertently dropped a tortellini on his tie at a business lunch. When someone pointed it out to him, he looked down, picked up his tie and licked it off. Emily Post must have spun in her eternal resting place.

Everything okay? Now your appointment can be made without distracting thoughts about having a piece of spinach caught between your teeth. There's no need to be self-conscious. You'll be able to walk into any room and concentrate on the people and business at hand.

An Entrance They Will Never Forget

Your 30-second Detail Check is complete. You may even be 15 minutes early because you are working on "Lombardi time." This meticulous coach had all his players set their watches ahead 15 minutes so that there was an immediate impression of being professional and respecting other people's time. Today, even five minutes is noted and appreciated.

Don't chew gum. Ever. There is probably not one single thing any of us could do to damage our initial impression more than chomping on chewing gum. Loudly sucking on candy is a close second.

If you are in a customer's reception area, don't spend too much time chatting with the receptionist. Just present your business card, be friendly, and indicate with whom you have an appointment.

It is fine to glance over a file or take out something business-oriented, compact, and easy to put away. But definitely don't take out a novel to read. A receptionist for a manufacturing firm told us that one vendor was so engrossed in her Stephen King book that she never even looked up when two vice presidents came into the reception area to greet her. They had to interrupt her and she began the first five seconds with a sheepish smile and an apology.

Try not to eagerly smile at everyone who enters the reception area. Keep a pleasant expression, but stay businesslike. Be prepared to shake hands and do it standing up, not seated.

The clock starts when you first make eye contact. You now have 60 seconds to transform a new acquaintance into a new associate, or 60 seconds to re-establish your relationship with an existing client. There is no need to hurry, rush, or do all the talking. This is the time to demonstrate your interest in them and your assurance in yourself.

> Good posture not only takes off 10 years and 10 pounds, it creates an instant impression of competence.

Confident people have a rhythm to their movements and an energy to their stride. Never poke your head around the corner in an apologetic gesture. If you walk into someone's office and a handshake is appropriate, stand far enough away from the desk so that the person must come from behind it to greet you. If you are the host, it is always more gracious to meet people in the reception area.

Good posture not only takes off 10 years and 10 pounds, it creates an instant impression of competence. If you get too physically tired at the end of the day, schedule important face-to-face meetings before 3:00 P.M. Sagging shoulders and slumping posture project defeat and exhaustion.

Make friendly, direct eye contact. One of the best exercises that we do in our seminars is to role-play an entrance. When the participants simulate the first entrance, the player makes eye contact, breaks it to look around the room, and then reconnects

A friend of ours met Robert Redford at an ice cream store in Montana. Just standing beside him in line made her light-headed and she nearly fainted. Composing herself as much as she could, she ordered her Rocky Road cone and paid her money. Walking outside, she discovered that she was so starstuck that she had forgotten her cone. When she went back inside the store, Robert Redford was still there. While she stood in line to retrieve her ice cream, he leaned over, smiled, and said, "If you are looking for your ice cream cone, it's in your purse."

for the handshake. This is generally how most of us greet each other.

The second time, the player makes eye contact and maintains it all the way to the handshake. Connection and confidence soar when eye contact is not broken. (A more thorough discussion of handshakes and eye contact appears in Chapter 4.)

Let Me Present to You . . .

As you shake hands, take the opportunity to address the other person by name and to repeat your own, "Ms. Carroll, I'm David Jason from United Telephone." Everyone loves the sound of his or her name. Repeating it flatters them and helps you remember it. It also gives you a simple way to correct someone else's mispronunciation of your own name.

Use a tag line. Never assume that the people you are meeting know who you are or why you are there. "I'm glad Doug Pepper was able to arrange this meeting. I think you'll find our Web site services to be exactly what you want."

If you are introducing others, remember the golden rule of introductions: "The most honored person is mentioned first." If you follow the sequence of the phrase, "Mr. President, I would like to present . . . " you will always have it right.

Since the most honored person is mentioned first, gender, age, and even rank are secondary. That means that if you are introducing your boss to a customer, the customer is mentioned first because he or she is the most important, even if your boss is a vice president and the customer is a junior associate. The introduction would be, "Dan Jefferson, this is my boss, Tom Dodge. Tom, Dan is one of my favorite customers and a big fan of our new pantyhose promotion."

When two people of equal rank are introduced, the woman is mentioned first. "Patty Smith, I would like you to meet Gibbon Bonner. Gibbon has worked in New York for ten years, so you two really have something in common."

When a man and a woman are introduced and he is the president of the firm and she is an administrative assistant of that same firm, the introduction would be, "Mr. Bridges, I would like you to meet Mary Mehoff. Mary does a wonderful job in our transportation department."

If you simply remember that you honor and give added recognition to the person who is first mentioned and you include a conversational tag line, introductions will be easy, connecting, and correct.

One Minute Later

That's it. Your 60 seconds are up. Let's take a look at what has been accomplished.

First, with body language, you have demonstrated that you are comfortable in business situations. You arrived early and well prepared, which is also a critical part of your nonverbal communication.

Second, with eye contact, friendliness, and great posture you have begun the process of developing mutual trust.

Third, you have demonstrated that being well organized and in control of your side of the meeting always elicits respect.

Fourth, you have significantly influenced the outcome because everything you have done so far showcases you as a consummate professional.

Please Be Seated

Proximity helps create comfort. Many executives have a small, round conference table in their office. It allows

I vividly remember when I was in tenth grade and I wanted to call a girl named Patty and ask her to a dance. I spent maybe twenty-eight hours rehearsing exactly what I was going to say. So when I actually made the call, I was pretty smooth. 'Hello, Dance,' I said. 'This is Patty. Do you want to go to the Dave with me?' Fortunately Patty grasped the basic thrust of my gist and agreed to go to the dance. This was a good thing because if she had shot me down, I would have been so humiliated that I would never have been able to go back to school.

—Dave Barry, humor columnist

them to talk to guests without dominating the "power perch," which is always at the head of the table.

If a conference room is suggested, direct the meeting there. It is more neutral, like a Geneva, Switzerland of business environments. A conference room also has fewer distractions, such as a ringing phone or people stopping by.

If the office features a couch and armchairs, select an armchair because a sofa is often tough to get in and out of and can create uncomfortable side-by-side seating problems.

One of our clients went into a prospective customer's office and after she accepted the offer for coffee, she was told that the coffee was all gone. So she agreed to a second offer of cola. The cola was then casually grabbed and drunk by her potential customer. He had turned what should have been a fundamental gesture of business hospitality into an awkward situation.

If your host stays behind a giant desk, just remember the experience with Buck and try to convene in another environment, perhaps the conference room. We have clients who always carry transparencies or a laptop presentation with them so that they can legitimately request that the meeting be moved into a training room or a conference room where screens and projection systems are available.

If your client offers you a beverage, accept it, even if you don't plan to drink all of it. A sip or two simply shows cordiality and friendliness. It also warms the atmosphere and lengthens the meeting. If you are the one offering, make sure you have the beverage available before you suggest it.

The awkward moment that comes when you have just sat down, but before serious discussion has started, makes an ideal time to exchange business cards. That practice is standard in Japan. The Japanese never wait until the end of the meeting for the ritual of exchanging cards.

The business card is part of your personal and corporate image. It should always be on excellent card stock, and the image it projects should be professional and in keeping with your industry. Generally black or blue ink on a buff or white card stock is considered to be the most appropriate. Add gold foil, blind embossing, an expertly designed logo, or more than two colors and your card will have more impact. Take the time and spend the money to have new information reprinted. Never give anyone a card with crossed-out information. Be sure to add e-mail and Web addresses.

Avoid listing post office boxes on your card unless you are part of a large and well-recognized company. It gives the impression of a company that is not large enough to have a business address.

Exchanging business cards is a good way to bring your new acquaintances "up to speed." The card will impressively present your name, title, and company with no errors. Better yet, the other people at the meeting will usually respond by presenting their cards, too. If someone from the other party has to leave the meeting before the session concludes, exchanging cards early gives everyone the information needed for later follow-ups.

> Talk to someone long enough so that you have a sense of whether you want him or her to be able to locate you. Make your card have value.

In presenting a business card professionally, don't become overeager. Don't act as though it is the first one you have ever presented. Be smooth—rooting around for one in a purse or a briefcase is bad form. Keep your cards in a convenient pocket or have them easily obtainable from your purse, briefcase, or card case.

At business meetings it is natural that everyone should have your card. But at cocktail parties, networking sessions, or on airplanes, don't pass your cards around like popcorn. Talk to someone long enough so that you have a sense of whether you want him or her to be able to locate you. Make your card have value.

Smile and the World Smiles Back

Try it. Smile. It works because it is almost impossible not to return one. We are programmed to imitate each other's behavior. A smile is one of the most important business tools we have, and the one we most frequently forget to use. The hurried pace of business and the intensity of situations often leaves us reflecting the same anxiety on our face. When we do team-building sessions, "humor and fun" are almost always listed as important team values. There are times when we all need to consciously remind ourselves to "lighten up."

Note that we're not talking about a forced, insincere grin. An easy, relaxed smile says that you enjoy your work and enjoy meeting people. That kind of smile puts everyone at ease.

Impressions from Start to Finish

The objective of the first impression is to start the process on a professional note. You sell yourself first, and *then* you sell your company and your product. Building rapport starts with the first impression, although you can't expect a permanent bonding. Only continued exposure will firmly establish trust, respect, and a lasting partnership.

In our office, we have individual Affirmation Jars. These are inexpensive pasta containers on each desk labeled with our name. We can write a quick note of appreciation, give someone movie tickets, a cartoon, a funny e-mail, a cigar, or leave a piece of candy as a follow-up thank you.

Finally, nothing destroys a good impression faster than overstaying your welcome. Your exit will be remembered! Wind things up quickly and don't linger. Shaking hands signals the end of a meeting. In less formal situations, if you initiate the end, make it friendly and fairly crisp with assigned action items and timetables.

Part of parting is the follow-up thank you. It can be e-mailed, handwritten, typed, or voice mailed. This is a very valuable component of establishing professional presence because so few people take the time to thank others. You will set yourself apart if you offer your thanks within 24 hours.

Lost Opportunity

We prefer to do business with people we trust and people we believe to be credible. Business is conducted at a frenzied pace and opportunities come and go quickly. Establishing an effective physical presence gives us a competitive advantage in today's fast-paced business world.

If, in that first 60 seconds when people are gathering information about us, we deliver solid, positive information about ourselves, there is a greater opportunity to move to the business at hand. Why give anyone data or evidence to doubt our intelligence, experience, and credibility?

Mary Johnson, a human resource professional for a hotel chain, was conducting interviews to fill a position for a maintenance manager at one of the properties. She was looking forward to her last interview of the day. The candidate's résumé reflected years of experience and the exact expertise she was looking for. Her hopes were quickly dashed.

He swaggered into her office 20 minutes late and didn't acknowledge it. He surveyed the office, barely greeted her, made little eye contact, and didn't offer to shake her hand. Without a care in the world he proceeded to plop, uninvited, into the most comfortable chair in the office. Hers. Being the consummate professional, she thought, "Perhaps he's just a little rough around the edges. I'm sure he's very bright and capable of doing the job." She gave him a chance and proceeded with the interview.

Fifteen minutes of questions was enough to reveal that he did possess the credentials outlined in his resume, but she couldn't get past the poorly made first impression. If he wasn't effective with her, how was he going to have the presence to lead and manage a staff of 20? She chose to hire someone else.

> Most H.R. training in interviewing skills is focused on trying to overcome the first 3 minutes of the interview and the emotions it creates. These emotions are so powerful and long lasting that they will affect hiring decisions, over-riding educational credentials and experience.

A Natural Attraction

Making a positive first impression is not fawning over someone, falsely flattering him or her, appearing subordinate and submissive, or trying to overpower them. A first impression should create a human connection that includes all parties and puts everyone on the same playing field. It will influence whether you land or lose a contract, get hired or overlooked for a job, or diffuse or increase conflict. Make those first 60 seconds count!

two

Developing the Art of Self-Promotion

In writing or speaking give to every person his due title according to his degree and custom of the place.

—*Manners, Culture and Dress, 1890*

Self-promotion is not the exclusive arena of public relations experts, high-profile business leaders, or millionaire sports stars. Proactive business professionals today view themselves as if they were incorporated and market their talents accordingly. Doing high-quality work is not enough. Just as a solid, viable product will die a slow death without consistent marketing, talented contributors can be ignored, overlooked, or never fully utilized without effective self-promotion.

> Just as a solid, viable product will die a slow death without consistent marketing, talented contributors can be ignored, overlooked, or never fully utilized without effective self-promotion.

One reason for this is the warp speed that everyone maintains. There is so much on everyone's radar screen. There aren't enough senior executives who stay around long enough to recognize all the talent of their team or to promote people internally. So the job of showcasing talent resides with each individual. If properly positioned, this isn't offensive hucksterism,

17

it's smart career-pathing. It's being accountable for the growth of your professional life.

There are many ways for companies to gain respect, market share, and media attention. Individual recognition comes from the same adept self-promotion. Both companies and individuals share the common characteristic that recognition rarely happens on its own.

> The business expands or shrinks in direct proportion to one's courage.

So self-promotion starts by overcoming shyness or feelings of inadequacy. Assess yourself honestly. Do you toil in the background, never having anyone champion you? Do you watch less talented people moving up in the organization? When interesting opportunities arise, are you overlooked? Chances are, you have unique problem-solving capabilities and achievements that have made a difference to both people and projects. These important contributions deserve to be showcased.

Blaming your status or situation on the company or your boss is usually pointless and unfortunately counterproductive. Whether we like it or not, in today's rapidly evolving business environment, we are the ones accountable for our own careers. We are responsible for asking for training, volunteering for projects that give us additional experience, and being continually vigilant in looking for beneficial career opportunities.

You Are More Quotable Than You Think

When one of our clients who owns a small business first moved to Seattle, she read a humorous column in the *Seattle Post-Intelligencer* about the demise of shoulder pads for women. The otherwise well-informed journalist thought they were ugly and deforming, so he was delighted that they were becoming unstylish.

Our client sat down and wrote a two-page letter, in a humorous tone, defending shoulder pads as a basic necessity for every woman who is smaller on top than on the bottom, which covers about 99 percent of women. A week later, on the front page of the Lifestyle section, her name started off his column.

This was her first step in becoming visible in a brand new city. The newspaper devoted an entire column to the letter she wrote. Even if she could have bought that much advertising space, it would not have generated as much positive attention and credibility as being quoted by a respected local columnist. It became clear to her that self-promotion isn't as complicated as it may appear, and that a large, prestigious publicity machine isn't always necessary. But it has to be done judiciously and with high credibility.

More Than 15 Minutes of Fame

Self-promotion is not just the few minutes of fame that Andy Warhol promised us. Self-promotion is much more extensive and useful than that. It is building long-term relationships and a good reputation, lobbying for a promotion, as well as positioning ourselves as a subject matter expert in our area.

The variety of self-promotion methods range from handing out business cards judiciously at a chamber of commerce networking session to being the keynote speaker for a national convention. But don't stop there. In addition to handing out business cards and receiving new ones, follow up with individuals with whom you found a common interest. A telephone call, voice mail message, or a short note will solidify the person's memory of you and continue the relationship.

Volunteering to deliver one presentation is just the beginning. Strategically choose a few events each year where you can deliver some kind of presentation in your area of expertise. It's important to choose the kinds of self-promotion that are consistent with your personality and your goals.

Sometimes overdone self-promotion is so obvious it becomes almost comic. When holiday cards were passed around a corporate office, each senior executive signed them, understanding that protocol indicated that the space underneath the imprinted corporate name would be saved for the president's signature. However, the head of operations, who was gunning for the presidential spot wrote his name under the imprinted company name. The president, who received the circulated cards last, ended up signing his name in the side margin.

Networking on the Up-and-Up

We've all witnessed it. He walks into the room, makes eye contact, confidently approaches a group, and introduces himself to each person. She's at every event you attend, is always smiling and full of energy, and leading interesting conversation. For some people, networking is a gift. For most of us, it is a learned skill vital to personal and professional growth.

Seventy-five percent of individuals within each group we deliver seminars to indicate that networking is the least favorite aspect of professional presence. No one denies that it is critical to business. But we hear comments such as, "Networking events are so phony and superficial," "Everybody is so focused on their own agenda it's nonproductive," "I can never come up with enough things to talk about," or "People only call you when they need something."

> Resolve to be tender with the young, compassionate with the aged, sympathetic with the striving, and tolerant with the weak and wrong . . . because sometime in your life you will have been all of these.
> —Common proverb

Let's face it. We've all been to events where we've been the victim of someone with their own agenda, someone who's cornered us for 30 minutes to talk only about themselves and how much business they are doing. We've all encountered the individual who, while pretending to be interested in what you have to say, is looking over your shoulder to find someone more interesting to talk to. Then there is the "master schmoozer" who has the reputation for promising great and wondrous things, but never follows up.

Like all other facets of business, networking is changing. Merriam-Webster defines networking as "the exchange of information or services among individuals, groups, or institutions." Practiced in the literal sense of the definition, networking can and should be a positive experience, not a negative one.

A colleague of ours advises not to "do networking" for the sake of networking. It's not about the network, it's about the people. Do it because you learn something from everyone you meet. You never know when you can help someone or when he or she can help you. Networking, put in the context of building relationships, can be fun.

It's not just about what you can do for others and what they can do for you. Networking is connecting other people who may have something in common. You will be remembered for helping other people make mutually beneficial connections.

Networking is a lifelong process. You can't just decide to attend an event or two and expect to see results. Networking pays off after years of establishing connections and investing in relationships. Teresa Owens, president of her own consulting firm, says she was able to start her own business because she was so well networked. She left corporate America without a clear idea of what to do next, attended one of her regular networking events, and let people know she was now working on her own. She left the event with two clients that jumpstarted her firm. Nine years in corporate America doing excellent work for clients, building relationships, and volunteering in the community established her credibility and reputation.

If networking isn't your favorite practice, start small. Be a resource for people in your company. We have a tendency to work only on our own projects and stay within our own department. Stretch to meet people in other departments. Find out what they are working on and what interests them. Figure out how you can provide information, expertise, or a contact to help them out or save some time.

Do a fundraising event for a worthy cause. One colleague shares some advice she received when just starting out. "Don't be intimidated by people's position in the company or their ability. If you show the person and the position respect, they will talk to you. They probably started in business the same way you did, working their way to the top."

Watch how expert networkers work a room. Shadow a friend or colleague that has a special expertise for building relationships. Observe how they approach people and engage in conversation. Listen to the way they ask questions and draw people out. Start by

One of our clients met an individual at a networking event who was doing research for a book about enhancing individual potential. The next day our client sent a simple e-mail to the individual indicating how nice it was to meet her at the event and included two resources for information on her topic. The individual later proved to be influential in getting our client's workshop into a client organization.

cultivating relationships with those who share your interests and values. Remember the people you meet, what they do, and their areas of expertise. The key to getting results through networking is to always follow up with people and to stay in touch. It is a small world. The more people you know, the more visible you are, and the stronger your business becomes.

Everyday Promotion Tactics

Self-promotion is not just for special times and special projects. Every time we greet people, voice an opinion at a meeting, or take a customer out for lunch, we are promoting ourselves. Here are six things you can do on an everyday basis:

1. Keep agreements and commitments. Nothing makes a more powerful statement of integrity and reliability than doing what we say we're going to do.
2. Keep business cards available at all times. Tuck several in your wallet and suit jacket, plus your coat pocket and briefcase. When someone asks for information, such as the name of your favorite restaurant in town, jot it down on your business card. Just make sure it isn't dog-eared. Over 30 million business cards are exchanged every day—it is the most common method of self-promotion.
3. Be certain that everyone in your neighborhood, your volleyball or tennis team, your church, and every club that you belong to knows exactly what you do for a living and how to locate you.

    To find out that someone you know through one of your organizations placed an order for one thousand computers with a competitor, listed his office building with another realtor, or hired another financial counselor because he or she didn't know that you were in that industry is a significant lost opportunity.

    This doesn't mean that you corner your neighbors at the community swim club with your brochure and a 30-minute presentation. What it does mean is that you let people know, in a friendly, nonthreatening way, exactly what you do. Asking them what business they are in becomes a fairly easy lead-in to disclose your business as well.

Certainly another way is to offer to do a free seminar or presentation to members of your organization. If you are a financial consultant, volunteer to speak to the "Singles' Class" at church about managing money. If you sell real estate, offer to do a breakfast meeting at the chamber of commerce on buying and selling property. If you sell athletic equipment and belong to a social club, volunteer to organize a "Sports Day" where you can display your sporting goods.

Members of Rotary Clubs, baseball teams, or the local synagogue will generally do business with people they know personally, *if they know what you do*. There is almost a guarantee that members will receive a fairer price and more personal service from another member than from a stranger.

4. Send appropriate letters of congratulations, thank-you notes, and news clippings on topics of interest to clients and colleagues on a regular basis. If you have just had a discussion on a particular stock and the next day there is an article about that company, clip it out and send it to extend the conversation and your mutual interest.

5. Make business referrals to clients and colleagues whenever possible. If you are comfortable with the caliber of someone's work, allow him or her to use your name.

One of the most elegant and disarming techniques is to cultivate your so-called competitors, make them your colleagues, and do cross-referrals with those whom you respect. Your willingness and ability to do this will set you apart from those in your field who come across as insecure and territorial.

6. Be accessible. Come early for the social hour prior to an event and don't immediately leave after a corporate dinner. Talk, mix, and mingle with colleagues and customers. Don't spend the entire evening telling everyone how tightly scheduled and

incredibly busy you are and that it is a miracle that you even found the time to be here! Make sure you graciously attend company picnics, birthday parties, and after-hours get-togethers as your schedule permits. Return phone calls promptly, and if you have moved from one department to another or left a company, stay in contact and be accessible to your former colleagues.

Even well-known people follow the rule of staying accessible. Dr. Joyce Brothers, for example, received a phone call from a small town newspaper in Alabama during an extensive promotional tour where every major network interviewed her. Despite her hectic schedule, she took the time, between media appearances, to return the phone call to the newspaper journalist, treating him exactly the way she would have treated an interview from the *New York Times*. She cultivated one more friend in the media, knowing that each reporter adds to the enhancement and credibility of her image and advice.

False Modesty Is Not a Virtue

It is not good business to wait for others to notice what's going on with you, or to expect others to publicly acknowledge your contributions. This is especially true for women. Research has proven that women's accomplishments are less acknowledged and less remembered than those of men.

As a matter of fact, false modesty is self-defeating. The person who always defers and lets others take the credit for his or her contribution gains little thanks and no respect. No one wants to be on a team with players of low self-esteem. When a project is a team effort, it is not only recommended but essential to give credit to everyone, including yourself.

If the project requires a presentation to a committee, volunteer to be the spokesperson. You will gain visibility even as you share the

A colleague, Al Nucifora, writes a weekly column for the local business journal that gives him immeasurable exposure to new and existing clients. He receives calls and e-mails every week from readers who are his target market. He adds each published article to his Web site. His columns are informative, straightforward, and offer excellent information. Al is viewed as a true subject matter expert because he is in print every week.

credit. If the boss seems to be hoarding all the glory, have a private conversation with him or her and request that you and the other team members have a chance for the limelight, too.

Suggest that photos be taken when your team contributed to an exciting event. Have the editor of the company newsletter do a story. When you chair a committee, make sure your name is listed on the program, along with those of the other committee members. If your company has a policy against that, then keep copies of any articles surrounding the program that mention your name.

If you are chairing a project for an organization such as Sales and Marketing Executives or the American Cancer Society, why waste an opportunity to get some valid name recognition? When you are the most important contributor, self-promotion is even more important. In fact, you will look weak and insecure if you toil like a workhorse, fully expecting to stay in the background. No one really appreciates a martyr.

If you have done a particularly good job with a client's project, ask for a letter acknowledging that fact. The appropriate time to do that would be when the customer is thanking you in person or on the phone. You might say, "I'm glad it worked, and that you liked the job I did. I'd sure appreciate it if you would put that in writing." Then request that the person send the letter to your boss or the CEO with a copy to you. Or just ask if you may use them as a reference in the future.

Recognition, Not Notoriety

The right attitude, a dose of subtlety, and a sense of perspective are vital to successful self-promotion. So is sensitivity to how others perceive you. No one likes the image of an insatiable publicity hound.

Self-promotion is not just a "Look how cool I am!" attitude. An executive recruiter invited a client of ours

Zsa Zsa Gabor certainly received a great deal of publicity, more than she could ever buy, with her "cop slapping" incident. But all it really produced was notoriety. It didn't generate any positive recognition. In fact, tee shirts that initially screamed "Free Zsa Zsa" changed to "Kill Zsa Zsa" within a week. Even Zsa Zsa herself said, "I am so famous, it's sickening!"

to his office where he had well over one hundred trophies, certificates, and plaques. Some were from his son's and daughter's soccer team. Others looked as though they had been purchased at a garage sale. Rather than giving him added credibility and visible credentials, the sheer number made him appear shallow and insecure, especially when he insisted on giving her a grand tour of the "Hall of Fame."

Several well-placed plaques, or tasteful gifts of recognition, can be a fine addition to a professional's office. Just as we get assurance from a doctor's office where there are impressive diplomas on the wall, we gain a sense of good citizenship of one whose office displays plaques of recognition from the March of Dimes, the Salvation Army, the local food bank, or the neighborhood baseball team. But office walls full of plaques or glass cases loaded with a child's soccer trophies give an indication of a possible self-esteem issue.

Office décor can be useful for self-promotion. Every office needs something that will begin conversation. A collection of wooden ducks or silver spoons, a stunning piece of art, a beautiful wall hanging, or an outstanding view of the city skyline can serve as an initial point of discussion.

Several nicely framed pictures of your family or friends are fine, but avoid unframed snapshots propped up by a pencil holder. A printer whom one of our clients formerly worked with displayed a nude picture with Kevin Costner's head pasted on it and a "personalized greeting" from Kevin. It showed questionable taste.

The familiar or romantic things that work so well in the home are out of place in an office. A large jewelry box, a lacy picture frame, or a nude statue are too personal. So are alluring glamour shots of your spouse or personal companion.

Copies of off-color jokes scotch-taped onto the wall can invite lawsuits. One poster quips, "I feel like a mushroom. They keep me in the dark and feed me s——." It may clearly express how one feels about the working environment, but it certainly doesn't set this individual on the top of the list for new projects or promotions. Nor does it set the right tone for clients and colleagues.

The cartoon *Dilbert* is very funny and sometimes so accurate it feels like Scott Adams is sitting in the cubicle next to us. It is also dedicated solely to a cynical look at business, and cynics rarely get promoted. Consider carefully before displaying too much *Dilbert*.

Make certain your office décor makes a statement that is congruent with your business presence and reflects the way you want to be perceived by others.

Writing Your Way to Success

One of the most effective ways to build or enhance a reputation is through the written word. For years, universities and colleges have insisted on the "publish or perish" doctrine. Although companies don't usually encourage it, they are certainly impressed when employees take the initiative to write and publish articles. It is not necessary to be a professional writer to submit an article for publication, just a competent one who has done the required homework. There are six ways to take advantage of the power of the pen.

> The cartoon *Dilbert* is very funny and sometimes so accurate it feels like Scott Adams is sitting in the cubicle next to us. It is also dedicated solely to a cynical look at business, and cynics rarely get promoted. Consider carefully before displaying too much *Dilbert*.

1. If you have read a great business book or attended a powerful, cutting-edge seminar or heard a terrific speaker, consider putting together a one- or two-page executive summary and e-mailing it to your boss, your colleagues, and maybe some selected customers.

2. Volunteer to write a regular column or quarterly article for your company newsletter. It is a terrific way to become more visible in your company. Those who publish the newsletter will be very grateful, since it is less copy for them to write.

   Don't just dash off some remarks off the top of your head. The printed word is permanent and public, so you don't want anything printed that will embarrass you later. Write as well as you can and be sure to check your facts. Have at least two colleagues proofread your article for content, style, and typos.

Keep in mind, too, that while a controversial subject or angle may gain you a lot of attention, it is likely to alienate more people than it will persuade or impress.

Ask the editor if your picture can be included. Be sure that you have a flattering, professionally photographed headshot on hand.

Inquire when your column will appear and how to secure copies. Watch for its publication and be sure to get extra copies of the published piece to keep for your business portfolio. Just as extracurricular activities are important to a college entrance committee, so too are activities that show your talents and motivation to do extra projects in the business world.

3. Call your industry trade journal to see whether they accept articles from outside sources. If they do, you will have a knowledgeable and captive audience for an article. You will gain important stature within your industry when you appear in a publication that is widely read by your coworkers, your competitors, and your boss.

   This exposure helps build your reputation as an expert. From computers to banking to medical care to image consulting, every industry has at least one trade journal where you can showcase your knowledge.

4. Create a one-page informational piece that your clients would enjoy reading. For instance, if you are in the convention business, you might put together a list of the best restaurants and boutiques in your city. If you sell cellular telephones, compile some amusing customer comments on the unusual ways that their mobile phone has impacted their business relationships.

   This "newsletter" can be mailed or e-mailed to your existing clients and prospective customers and used as an informational piece for any presentation that you do. If it is in written form, be sure it is printed on your letterhead and that your name appears on the document.

   If you use the e-mail format, either send notification to the receiver that includes a link to your Web page where the newsletter resides or send the newsletter in the text of the e-mail. It is not always easy for the receiver to download an attached document if they don't have compatible software, so keep the format and the font simple. It doesn't benefit you or leave a favorable impression if a client or colleague has to work too hard to open and read an e-mail.

5. When you have been promoted, elected to serve as an officer on a board, or have won an award, type up a simple one-page press release, and send it to your daily newspaper in care of the editor of the business section along with a black-and-white glossy headshot. Also send the same release and photo to your weekly business journal. If there are any trade journals that regularly publish information about individuals, be sure to send them a press release, too.

A press release should be done on your letterhead and should look something like this:

For immediate release
Contact: Janet Deans
(404) 623-9000

JANET DEANS ELECTED
TO MILLION-DOLLAR CLUB
FOR HER OUTSTANDING SALES RECORD

Janet Deans was recently made a member of this year's Million-Dollar Club for selling over one million dollars worth of real estate in the Atlanta area. She has been with the Ben Bridges Real Estate firm for the past two years and is past president of the New Realtor's Club in Dunwoody. This is the second year that Ms. Deans has won this award.

Ms. Deans will be recognized at the annual awards dinner at the Ritz Carlton on May 12.

6. For maximum exposure, write a book. If that seems overwhelming, then write a booklet in your area of expertise. A booklet can work as an important handout in a company

training course or could easily be disseminated at industry trade shows. If your company won't pay for the printing cost, consider investing in the printing yourself. Real estate agents, financial planners, medical personnel, and other service-related professionals gain a substantial competitive edge with a short, well-written booklet that is chock full of information.

Writing takes time and discipline but the rewards are significant. You will be immediately perceived as an expert in your field. You will have credibility if you are looking for speaking opportunities, a promotion, or a new job.

A friend of ours in human resources ran an ad for an opening in his department. He was extremely impressed when he received not only a resume but also a copy of the candidate's 50-page booklet on effective recruiting. This candidate's name was at the top of the list when personal interviews were set up.

Making Friends with the Media

Media exposure is the most powerful way to gain attention, credibility, and clout. Whether the interview is with a newspaper or magazine, or you are being featured as an expert on radio or television, the impact and promotional potential are unlimited. When one source finds you interesting, usually others will, too.

One of our colleagues was involved in a program where she was teaching blind women how to apply makeup. A simple phone call to the local newspaper's Lifestyle editor was all it took to get a feature article.

Often it is as easy as picking up the phone and calling the editor or a reporter at your daily newspaper. Offer to be interviewed if you have done, or are doing, something newsworthy or can offer a valid perspective on a current issue.

Once you have established a relationship with a journalist, make certain you stay in contact. Drop them an occasional letter, mail them a holiday card, or send an idea for an article with your business card. They will think of you as a valuable person to quote when they are doing a story on robotics, political candidates, hot-air ballooning, cosmetics, or whatever your specialty is.

To create opportunities for TV appearances, ask colleagues what local news programs they watch. Personally research all network and cable stations to see where the best fit would be for your expertise. If you have an idea, make an appointment with the station manager. The media is constantly looking for ways to keep their scheduling fresh and entertaining.

A physician in Atlanta created an opportunity with a phone call and a subsequent meeting. "Ask the Doctor" was a radio program that ran on Sunday afternoon for one year and brought the on-air doctor both name recognition and a thriving practice.

> A physician in Atlanta created an opportunity with a phone call and a subsequent meeting. "Ask the Doctor" was a radio program that ran on Sunday afternoon for one year and brought the on-air doctor both name recognition and a thriving practice.

To get on local radio programs, listen to see which station has the format that is suitable for what you want to offer. Then call the station and begin your fact-finding.

Susan Shulman of Leadership Training Associates, Inc. proposed to a large radio station a series of three-minute informational spots that could be aired during drive time. She interviewed local business professionals about tips for success, and her spots ran regularly during prime time. Getting the best results with the media means that you phone first and connect with a program director, a reporter, or the interviewer on a talk show. Then send your "hook," which is a clever, unusual angle that will grab viewers' attention. It may be tying your expertise to a current event or presenting a nontraditional point of a view on an issue of general interest.

They Want You . . . Now What?

Once you have danced your way into the hearts and minds of the media, you will probably be terrified of the opportunities you have created for yourself. The first time you are on the air, you probably won't sleep a wink the night before.

The first time a good friend was on a local morning television program, it was a disaster. She was so tired from thrashing around all night, worrying that her alarm wouldn't go off, that when it did go off at 4:30 A.M., all she wanted to do was go back to bed. But there she was at the studio at 6:00 A.M., setting up all her demonstration items while the technician was wiring her for sound.

"Three, two, one, you're on," and so she was. She did her first television interview with pearls clanging against her microphone, her skirt hitched too high, and demonstration items falling off the table. Afterward, all of her friends watched the video of her segment. It was so bad, it looked like a "Weird Al Yankovic" parody. But once we all stopped laughing, she learned from this experience and did a more professional job on her second appearance.

Whether you are on radio, television, or are being interviewed by the print media, here are five ideas that we have developed over the past 20 years of working with the media.

1. Narrow the focus of your interview. Decide beforehand what is the most interesting part of your product, your experience, or your company. Don't try to explain everything. It is usually only possible to make one or two points well, unless you are the subject of an extended article or live interview. Also work to tie it into a current trend.

2. Ask your media contact if they want visuals. Be ready with photos, horizontal slides, or actual demonstration items. "Talking heads" are usually boring, and a photo always adds to any printed articles.

   Plan your outfit well. Choose blue as your primary color because it is the most telegenic on camera. Before your appearance, sit down in front of a full-length mirror so you will know exactly how you will look in front of the camera. If the station doesn't have a professional makeup artist, hire one yourself. Most television stations will have a list of makeup artists. If not, a phone call to a local professional photographer will produce at least two or three names. If this will be national exposure, hire an image consultant to coordinate your total look. You will be much more pleased with your appearance.

3. In the printed media, you have little control over what will be printed and how you will sound. Make friends with the interviewer and express your concerns. When our firm was interviewed over a controversial firing of a female partner in a large firm because of her inappropriate image, we had to be careful that our views were expressed clearly. Although she was extremely competent and kept most of her long-term clients happy, she smoked, drank, and swore in front of them as well as her internal customers. Her firm viewed this as highly unprofessional behavior.

    We asked the interviewers not to distort our viewpoint to make it appear that we were judging this woman without having met her. We wanted to be quoted in a general sense and did not feel comfortable commenting on the specifics of her situation. What we did say was that smoking, swearing, and exaggerated "male" or "female" behavior doesn't enhance anyone's presence. We also said that fair or not, women in business could be reviewed more harshly for exactly the same behavior that is exhibited in men. In every case, the journalist respected our request to keep our remarks objective and to present a balanced viewpoint.

4. Frankness is refreshing, but total candor is a mistake. In the blush of a good interview, many have revealed personal information that was later regretted. Most savvy subjects have also found that it isn't necessary to directly answer every

John F. Kennedy, in his first-ever televised presidential debate, knew the value of looking good. He had spent six months campaigning in California in a convertible with the top down. His sun-streaked hair and tanned skin gave him a healthy, vigorous, athletic look. He dressed impeccably in an expensive, hand-tailored wool suit, crisp white shirt, and conservative silk tie. He hired a professional makeup artist and had television training. The results have gone down in media history. In a one-hour debate, he gained 21 percentage points.

question. Both the interviewer and the interviewee have the power to redirect the interaction.

5. If you generate successful media coverage, and want more, capitalize on the exposure. Send a copy of the interview or article that featured you plus your background data to other radio stations, TV stations, newspapers, and magazines. If one source has found your expertise worthy of exposure, the others often want to jump on the bandwagon.

Speaking Up to Speak Out

The easiest way to become visible in your company and community is to polish up your speaking skills and speak out! If you have the chance to get up in front of a large group to give a three-minute announcement about an upcoming event, do it. If you have the opportunity to present at a planning session, retreat, or dinner event, do it. If your company has a public relations firm or a speaker's bureau, let them know you are interested in being a company spokesperson in the community.

> Every activity of our lives is a communication of sort, but it is through speech that we assert our distinctiveness from other forms of life. Business, social and personal satisfaction depend heavily on our ability to communicate clearly to others what we are, what we desire and what we believe.
> —Dale Carnegie, *The Quick and Easy Way to Effective Speaking*

According to research polls, the greatest fear most people have is the terror of having to speak in public. That is one reason that good speakers are highly valued and well paid. But most are not born with speaking skills. This is largely a learned skill that gets better with practice. Dale Carnegie Training, Toastmasters International, public speaking seminars, and individual training will enhance your skills.

No matter where you live, there are dozens of clubs and organizations that use outside speakers on a regular basis. If you have a topic of interest, call the program chairperson and ask to address the group. The Internet is a good place to find out some of the basic data about local clubs.

Become active in your professional organizations and other business groups. Often these provide opportunities for greater involvement, including public speaking.

Holding a part-time political position is also an effective way to increase your name recognition, while contributing something to your community. Even in a small town, the mayor and the council or school board members have name recognition. Lawyers, doctors, dentists, accountants, insurance and real estate agents, and other businesspeople of all types have advanced their careers through public office.

Creative Self-Promotion

The art of self-promotion has nothing to do with boasting, bragging, or being obnoxious and pushy. The art of self-promotion is simply getting positive attention for yourself, your company, or your pet project with flair and professionalism.

> The art of self-promotion has nothing to do with boasting, bragging, or being obnoxious and pushy.

When one of our clients worked for a charity organization, she wanted to get the labor unions in Ohio involved in her fundraising. Although they had never been a part of our client's foundation, the unions were generous to other charitable causes.

After a dozen phone calls and several business lunches, she found out the name of the key person who could open doors for her. Then she found out what meetings he attended, secured an invitation, and introduced herself to him with a handshake, a business card, and an invitation to lunch the next day.

During the lunch discussion, he explained that he had never been personally approached by anyone from her foundation. Because of the tremendous number of members he could tap, they had the biggest charitable wine auction ever. All it took was a little self-promotion.

Take the Credit

Be accountable for getting credit for your accomplishments. Take responsibility for asking to be on a committee, speaking to a group, or writing an article.

Create your own opportunities for media exposure, even if they aren't directly related to your business. If you work for a large company that has its own public relations department, but they aren't interested in using you, secure your own spot on local television discussing hobbies like ocean kayaking, home remodeling, or anything else that you have proficiency in. Being noted as a martial arts expert, a proficient Japanese gardener, or a competitive rock climber gives dimension to you professionally and allows other people to recognize and acknowledge you through your outside interests.

Boasting and bragging are not effective methods of self-promotion. Delivering the goods is. Develop a reputation as someone who is willing to get in front of a group and offer a clever introduction for a speaker, contribute to a newsletter, chair a project, or talk to the media. It will pay off in generating many professional opportunities.

> Boasting and bragging are not effective methods of self-promotion.

three

3

Contemporary
Business Behavior

*In private watch your thoughts; in your family watch your
temper; in society watch your tongue.*

—*Manners, Culture and Dress, 1890*

A client's neighbor, Linda A., who had accidentally cut off
another car when she entered the highway, became enraged
when the whole carload of passengers made a rude hand gesture in unison to retaliate. Their utility vehicle had Linda's company's emblem on the side, so it was obvious they worked for the
same employer. She sped up, got their license number, and reported
them to personnel the minute she got to work.

When the driver was contacted, he admitted to what they had
done and apologized. But Linda wanted written letters of apology
from everyone who was in the car, and she wanted copies put in their
personnel files. The incident continued to accelerate until the whole
company knew about it.

When she told her other neighbors about this, she added, "They
were sure lucky that it was me they made that nasty gesture to. With
someone else from the company, it would have been a lot worse."

Most of her neighbors were extremely grateful that they were not
the "lucky" passengers in that vehicle. They also didn't understand

why she wouldn't let the matter drop and move on to more important issues. Being one of those people who is chronically unhappy with the way the world behaves, she generally majored in the minors, making big issues out of relatively small ones.

We live in an imperfect world full of flawed human beings. People are sometimes rude. We can't control the way others act and behave. Self-righteously trying to correct every grievance is pointless and nonproductive. Pointing out each indiscretion, rudeness, and slight is a waste of time and energy. Seeking to rise above poor manners is a much easier way to live, and it also epitomizes professionalism and presence.

> Rocks come with the farm.
> —David Deans, President of the industrial computer business, Rockwell Automation

Good manners are one of the hallmarks of professional presence. It is impossible to be considered sophisticated, well bred, and competent without them. No matter what our background, whether our parents schooled us in etiquette or not, as professionals it is our obligation to fill in the blanks in our lives and be generous enough to overlook the flaws in others.

A Chauvinist Pig? I Think Not.

Gender issues are usually muddled for men and sometimes are for women, too. One of the questions that is frequently raised in our seminars by male attendees is, "Can I show good manners to my female colleagues and clients without appearing sexist?" The answer is yes, yes, and again, yes.

For most women, the issue is simply that we don't want to be regarded as a nuisance. When a speaker constantly makes reference to the sole female in the audience, that speaker is treating her in a way that makes the audience annoyed, and her a clear nuisance.

Speakers are notorious for being inadvertently sexist. "Lady and gentlemen" is a silly way to start a presentation. Constantly making reference to the one or two women in a seminar is a mistake. In a meeting, it is completely unnecessary for a male to say, "I want to tell an off-color joke, but I wouldn't want to offend the woman in our group." Either tell the joke or don't tell it, but don't make the woman responsible for the behavior.

Women also don't want to be regarded as people who need special assistance simply because of their gender. Expressing good manners means that we lend a helping hand when the situation warrants it without gender consideration. Helping someone on with their coat, holding a door, or offering to carry something is not gender specific.

If a woman feels that a gesture is truly superfluous, she can simply say with a warm smile, "Thank you, I can manage myself." This will be a clear indication that well-bred courtesies were offered and she has decided to decline them. But rarely will genuine courtesies ever be refused—by men or women.

It is not advisable, however, to make a business encounter feel like a date. It is not necessary for a man to hold a chair for a female colleague, open and close her car door, stand up when she leaves the table, or create any gratuitous physical contact. The only exception would be in a formal dining environment. Then holding a chair at dinner and standing up if she leaves the table is considered excellent form.

Honey, Baby, Darlin'

It is never smart or useful to make a fuss in public over an unintentional gender mistake. A courtly older gentleman may rush to open the door for a woman, address her as ma'am, and maybe even slip with a "honey" or two.

As a woman, keep business objectives in mind. Accept the courtesies while keeping friendly, no-nonsense eye contact and a straightforward but open manner. But don't smile too much. Gracefully handling this situation shows that you have a sense of when and when not to make an issue of things.

When one of our clients was pregnant, she enjoyed continuing to attend a step aerobics class throughout her nine months. However, in one class, the instructor kept making references to how she could modify a particular routine to accommodate her pregnancy. Two of the super jocks in front of her turned around and hissed, "I wish you weren't in this class. This added instruction is driving us nuts." She hadn't requested extra assistance from the instructor, but in an ill-conceived attempt to include her, he alienated his participants and made her the brunt of their resentment.

As a man, it is safe to assume that businesswomen will not readily respond to terms of endearment like "baby" and "hon." As a woman, assume that younger businessmen will not favorably respond to "boy," "sweetie," or "darlin'" unless you have both the style and the relationship to carry it off.

A Public Mistake

A colleague was speaking at a sales award banquet and noticed the difference in how saleswomen were greeted on stage versus how salesmen were acknowledged. When a woman walked on stage to accept her award for exceeding her sales quota, she was hugged, kissed, and generally treated like a blushing bride.

When a man accepted the same award, his hand was shaken, his award presented, and that was it. No hugging, no kissing. He was treated like a professional receiving an award for hard work.

Many of the attendees, both male and female, were up in arms after the ceremony because of the way the awards were handled. The implication was that the saleswomen had gotten to the top because of their femininity and good looks and the men through their hard work.

The master of ceremonies thought that he was showing warmth and good manners in greeting the female award winners with an embrace. What he didn't realize was that good manners dictated that he should have disregarded gender and treated each person individually.

> One of our clients entered a law office where the partners were crouched behind the chairs of the conference room shooting each other with squirt guns. They had just won a major case and this was their way of releasing tension and celebrating. Although he thought it was pretty funny, he also decided not to use that particular firm.

Humor—Within the Bounds of Good Taste

Humor is a wonderful business tool and a way of lightening up the pressures of the workplace. It relaxes people and eases tensions, along with aiding a number of involuntary physiological functions like reducing high blood pressure and adding those feel-good serotonins to the bloodstream. Humor, however, must be used appropriately and within the bounds of good taste.

In business it is easy to let things get out of hand at a staff meeting or even a gab session in the hallway. Screeching and loud laughter are disruptive. Practical jokes are counterproductive.

Developing a sense of when to pull back and refocus on business is vital not only in showing good manners but also in maintaining power and control. To gain a reputation as the office clown without balancing this with a serious sense of direction is a mistake.

One of our seminar attendees worked with a colleague who had a sense of humor that was consistently scatological and offensive. "Watch out for Number One and don't step in Number Two" was his trademark joke. He was rarely taken seriously at staff meetings, and everyone was nervous about having him meet customers and vendors.

Managers in particular must be careful that their humor doesn't diminish the importance of a job, assignment, or new product. In that kind of environment, hard work and dedication can feel almost foolish. Staying late to check figures and polish up a report seems a waste of time if the boss cracks a bad joke about it.

One of the challenges of business is familiarity and establishing appropriate boundaries. While we want to get as close as possible to our customer, there are times when things can get uncomfortable. If a client or prospect starts telling a joke that is sexist, racist, or vulgar, be diplomatic but make your opinion known. The alternatives can be silence, changing the subject, or, if you are fairly close with the individual, simply saying that "I know that you really don't feel that way and please understand that I don't either." In the final analysis, the customer will end up respecting your position more.

Most of us in the training and speaking profession have sat through a great many presentations. Some are good. Some aren't. A few are outstanding. And almost all of them are too long. One of our favorite clients hands out two Nerf guns to members of his staff during strategic planning sessions. They are instructed to use them when the speaker is five minutes over his or her allotted time. Then the sharpshooters come out and the agenda is maintained. Clearly this works only when everyone is from the same company and shares a similar sense of fun.

Handling Anger on the Job

Professional presence means having credibility. We need for others to trust us and to feel our behavior is predictable. It's hard to trust or depend on someone who seems emotionally unstable and shows it through erratic or passive-aggressive behavior, excessive moodiness, or uncontrolled outbursts.

Of course, everyone blows up from time to time. We all have our hot buttons. Some issues simply ignite us and left unchecked, can produce behavior that is emotional and generally unprofessional. We need to know what these issues are so that we can begin to control our responses.

> If others see us frequently react irrationally to small matters, we will damage our influence with them in larger issues. In such cases, we are perceived as less than professional, less able to handle ourselves. Temper tantrums rarely enhance stature.

If others see us frequently react irrationally to small matters, we will damage our influence with them in larger issues. In such cases, we are perceived as less than professional, less able to handle ourselves. Temper tantrums rarely enhance stature.

Business professionals who begin to use foul and vulgar language whenever they are upset are easily pegged. They are making their anger obvious and transparent. It is easy to gauge their level of frustration by the number of times they swear in each sentence.

Similarly, the man or woman who frequently gets teary-eyed when a manager or client doesn't like his or her work is seriously jeopardizing a career. We are all entitled to an occasional cry at work, but with the door—or the bathroom stall—shut. Crying is an emotional display that doesn't win points or admiration, and crying out of frustration is far different than crying from a devastating personal or national tragedy.

One caveat to this is communicating to a selected few when you are going through a devastating personal crisis—the imminent or recent death of a child, spouse, parent, or other close relative. Presented as a means to elicit pity or special treatment probably isn't the best approach. However, allowing others to know when tragic, personal concerns are part of one's life allows for a margin of compassion and understanding.

I'm Mad As Hell and I'm Not Going to Take It Anymore

Know your anger and frustration "triggers." Identify what turns you into a raving maniac. Awareness can then lead to a more responsible reaction. How many of these set you off?

Fourteen Surefire Anger Triggers

1. Being micromanaged.
2. Being criticized on a voice mail or e-mail and having it broadcasted.
3. Having a boss or colleague regularly critique your appearance.
4. Being on time and consistently waiting for the same people to show up late.
5. Being deliberately lied to.
6. Having to overhear the people in the cubicles next to you listen to their messages on speakerphone.
7. Discourteous treatment of any of your valued team members by other departments, customers, or outside vendors.
8. Watching a coworker show flagrant disregard of established rules and getting away with it.
9. Always being asked to do the "household chores."
10. Working with someone who refuses to admit mistakes.
11. Dealing with someone who constantly interrupts you in meetings and conversations or finishes your sentences for you.
12. Listening to endless personal chatter about subjects not related to business.
13. Having a confidence betrayed.
14. Having someone make you look inept, uninformed, or stupid in front of others.

There are many effective ways to respond to problems other than by getting angry or emotional. Here are three methods of handling your own anger on the job while maintaining a professional presence.

Method One: The Impassive Face

Rather than getting defensive and angry, don't react at all. Keep all signs of anger under wraps. When we observe some of our greatest business leaders, many, under circumstances of great anger, remain controlled. "The less said the better" is their style.

A powerful leader can select the appropriate emotion.

Of course, you can't keep anger pent up forever. It's not healthy. But choose the right way to deal with it. You can deal with the offender in private, vent your anger through exercise, or pour out your soul to a close, nonbusiness-related friend.

Method Two: The Patient Face

Sometimes in a flash of anger we react too quickly. We don't stop to listen or to let others finish their sentences. Something may hit us where we are vulnerable, and we check out of the logical, predictable world and travel on raw emotion.

If we can be patient and wait for the right moment, our anger can be better directed and channeled effectively. Our body language may still indicate that we are displeased, but in waiting to respond verbally, we create a more balanced response. Again, we appear to be in control.

The old tactic of counting to 10 can be very powerful. Sit or stand perfectly still. Work hard to put yourself in the other person's shoes. Look the person in the eye for several seconds. When you do begin to speak, speak slowly and quietly, carefully weighing your words. Make others strain a little to hear you. If your assailant is your boss, the same advice will help you maintain your dignity.

Method Three: The Funny Face

Consider lightening up. Help yourself by putting the situation in perspective. Do some self-talk. Is this really a deal-breaker? Poking a little fun at yourself and the circumstances will help you feel better, and everyone around you will be put at ease.

When You're on the Receiving End of Anger or Criticism

Class is often defined as grace under pressure. In each of our lives, there comes a time when we suffer some type of business humiliation. Depending on the business, it may happen more than once. There are a number of ways to react, most of which just worsen the problem.

Here is a list of the ways *not* to react to criticism:

1. *Make excuses*. "I haven't been feeling well lately, and you just keep making me work late. It's no wonder that I botched that project. I'm just exhausted."

2. *Cry*. "I know you don't like me. You have never taken me or my work seriously. You love to humiliate me in front of the office and make me cry."

3. *Counterattack*. "Well, I may not have gotten this report in on time, but at least I didn't get drunk and make a fool of myself at the last company picnic!"

The best way to defend yourself is often a completely straightforward, sincere apology. It will go a long way in rectifying the situation. Once you state, "I'm sorry. It's my fault," the discussion usually ends. When you step up and accept the blame for your behavior, others aren't so quick to blame or criticize you.

When You Are Attacked Publicly

Sometimes we are the object of a public attack and we can't really fight back. Not everyone has a good boss with a sense of timing, and certainly we can't control a public dressing down by a client or customer.

One of the best strategies for dealing with a situation in which you feel you have very little control is to use nonverbal behavior. If someone attacks you during a presentation and it would be too awkward to get up and leave, look the person squarely in the eye, hold the look for a moment, and then pick

> Focus on the solution, not the problem.

One of our clients, Ben, had spent many hours working on his sales presentation for the annual planning session. During his presentation, Ben's boss worked on his laptop nearly the whole time, only glancing up occasionally. Ben alternated between feeling angry and being distracted. As a result, his presentation wasn't nearly as smooth, cohesive, or effective as it could have been. During a break, he blew up at his boss, but did it privately. Although his boss was initially taken aback, their relationship actually improved. More open communication was established and his boss realized that staying glued to his laptop while his staff was presenting was not the best way to support his team.

right back up. Then your message becomes, "I heard you, but what you are saying is so off track and uncalled for that I choose not to deal with it." You will keep control of the situation and actually enhance your own power.

Reacting without having time to construct your case can be a mistake. Why get dragged into an unfriendly arena? In the heat of the moment, the less said the better. Showing little or no reaction can actually take the wind out of an angry sail, and you will end up the better player with more poise and presence. You can always reintroduce the issue later, with just the two of you, when tempers are more under control.

If a colleague, a superior, or even a customer has criticized you in public, it is always possible to take him or her aside later and to quietly say: "Please don't criticize me in public. If you have any criticism to make, tell me about it privately." Most bullies are so taken aback by a straightforward approach that they often change their behavior immediately.

Although discussing issues in private poses the least amount of conflict, this doesn't mean that you allow outright lies or misrepresentations to go publicly unchallenged. If the situation is critical to your integrity and other people are present, you may have to respond right then and there.

"Mike, you are misinformed. We did not let you down. We did not commit to a September fifteenth deadline because we need at least two weeks to ship, even on a rush order. This order wasn't even signed until September twelfth."

But choose carefully when to take up the gauntlet and when to let the other person just rant and play out the anger. It also allows you time to formulate your well-reasoned response.

An angry person is the one who is losing control. Often, the calmer you remain, the more absurd the other person appears. If you refuse to be drawn into the fray, your opponent looks increasingly ineffective.

Who Asked Your Opinion, Anyway?

When it comes to offering unsolicited advice, your best bet is to steer clear. This is true in the office as well as at social events. Even solicited advice is tricky. When someone asks what you think about their new office furniture, they usually don't want negative feedback no matter what they say. If you think it looks bizarre, overdone, or is just not your taste, why say anything?

> I'll be the coach not the critic.
> —Marry Morrow
> Executive Coach

The only time to call negative attention to someone's appearance or behavior is if they can do something about it immediately. Quietly mentioning that they have barbecue sauce on their forehead is a kind remark. Most people will feel grateful. Telling someone that their suit is much too tight or that their hairpiece looks like "road kill" is unnecessary.

In business conversation, is it correct to point out errors that other people have made? Of course. Data must be accurate and information clear. But this should be done without making the offender feel defensive. "I think you have those figures wrong, Fred. Let me show you what I have," is much better than, "Wrong, wrong, wrong. You always mess up those weekly sales figures."

Consideration in the Office

One of our clients complained that she was amazed at how unschooled her new recruit was in office protocol and basic consideration. She had scheduled a meeting with him for 1:00 and he kept her waiting until 1:30 P.M. because he had to drive home and "put the dog out."

"I know that he was being truthful in telling me why he was late, but I couldn't believe that he expected me to appreciate the fact that his dog took precedence over a meeting with me, his new boss. It was an immediate indicator to me to look for other problems. If he demonstrated such inconsiderate behavior toward me now, how was he going to treat our customers?"

Subsequently our client had a private conversation with her associate and pointed out his lack of consideration. She told him that his attitude and manners were just as important to the company as the actual dollars that he generated because, in fact, one lead to the other.

Being inconsiderate can also take the form of telling a business associate personal information that will make them resentful. Reporting to the harried receptionist that you will be gone for three hours because you are going to exercise and then enjoy a full-body massage is insensitive at best. If you are leaving the office for some type of personal enjoyment during office hours, it's a breach of good office etiquette to create potential resentment by revealing your destination to someone who doesn't have the same opportunity.

Where There's Smoke . . .

The etiquette of smoking today is simple. Don't do it in front of other people, unless everyone is outside and everyone is smoking. It used to be a shared experience—a meeting over a cup of coffee and a cigarette—but no more. Smoking in public is almost like using a toothpick; it is best done alone or with others in a designated smoking area. The exception is the Martini and Smoke Bar where it is assumed that exceptional hand-rolled cigars are enjoyed with a cocktail.

> Smoking in public is almost like using a toothpick; it is best done alone or with others in a designated smoking area.

However, if you are taking colleagues or clients, make certain that everyone will enjoy a cigar, not just a chosen few. For nonsmoking individuals who especially dislike cigars, it is hard to imagine a worse night than being in a smoked-filled room that is saturating their freshly cleaned business suit, watching scores of smokers light up cigars.

Five Misfires in the Smoking Arena

1. Don't smoke in restaurants, even in the smoking section, unless everyone else is smoking at your table, too.
2. Don't smoke in your own car if you are heading to an appointment. The odor will be very apparent even with the windows rolled down. Smoke attaches to clothing and the breath of a smoker so it "hits" others immediately.
3. Don't wear the same suit the day after you have gone to a smoky bar. Even if you don't smoke and even if you air out the suit overnight, it will smell of smoke. Most all-wool garments need 24 hours of freshening.
4. Don't miss washing your hair after an evening with smokers because it also retains the odor.
5. Don't smoke cigars unless you are outside or in a cigar bar.

> If you do smoke, you have the right to do it. Just use the utmost courtesy in business situations.

If you do smoke, you have the right to do it. Just use the utmost courtesy in business situations.

Attitude Adjustment

Whatever you do in the name of business, whatever courtesies you extend, must be offered with integrity and not grudgingly. Your enthusiasm and graciousness must be genuine.

If you feel that you dislike doing business with people from other cultures, with women, obese people, homosexuals, older people, or other minorities and your manner and attitude reflects that, you need an attitude adjustment. When such discrimination is flagrant, it is against the law. When it is more subtle, it is counterproductive to business.

Then there are issues that reside in behavior. Loud people, moody people, womanizers, harmless flirts, whiners, or overly macho men may really annoy you. But if you must deal with them, address your feelings first. Aside from being fair, it's also just good business.

We are able to select our friends. We usually don't have the opportunity to select our customer base. The success of our business encounters will depend on our ability to make a genuine connection without hostile or condescending undercurrents.

Good manners are not just reserved for those who share the same values. In a business relationship, courtesies need to be extended to everyone. Find a way to put aside your judgments and seek an authentic area of mutual interest or concern.

Roberta Langford is a well-educated colleague who was raised in a rather privileged and sheltered background. As a sales manager for a large chemical company, she often takes out groups of what she considers to be unsophisticated manufacturer's representatives who tend to discuss women's anatomy and violent movies over dinner.

> Good manners are not just reserved for those who share the same values. In a business relationship, courtesies need to be extended to everyone.

She used to dread their monthly visits but was usually unsuccessful in getting out of the obligation. So she decided to do something about it.

The first thing she made herself do was mentally place her poor attitude in the glove compartment of her car before walking into the restaurant. Second, she mentally placed a large sign around the neck of each man that said, "I am a caring, concerned human being who loves my family."

Third, she took charge of the conversation by asking her customers questions until she found something that they all enjoyed discussing. As it turned out, two of the men felt as strongly as she did about the importance of preserving the environment. In fact, one of them had organized a neighborhood recycling center.

Finding this area of mutual interest surprised her. She now sincerely looks forward to spending the evening together with them when they're in town. She also became comfortable enough to let them know when they overstep the bounds in sexual or sexist discussion.

They eventually confided to her that the only reason they used to have dinner with her was to get a free meal in a great restaurant. They had perceived her as stuffy and arrogant. Now that they found out that she was spending one Saturday a month picking up trash along the highway, she was a "regular guy" to them. Roberta decided, because of this experience, that if she was going to consider herself a professional, she should be able to show a level of graciousness whether or not she liked a client personally.

> Good manners are a show of respect. They humanize and harmonize business relationships, and promote a powerful spirit of cooperation in our work environments.

Good Manners Are Not a Meaningless Ritual

Etiquette for etiquette's sake is an empty activity and a meaningless ritual. But genuine good manners and a working knowledge of professional behavior are essential and productive business skills. Good manners are a show of respect. They humanize and harmonize business relationships, and promote a powerful spirit of cooperation in our work environments.

Step Two

Establish Effective Nonverbal Communication

four

The Language of Presence, Posture, Handshakes, and Eye Contact

To gain the good opinion of those who surround them, is the first interest and the second duty of men in every profession of life. For power and for pleasure, this preliminary is equally indispensable.

—*Manners, Culture and Dress, 1890*

Dr. Albert Mehrabian, in his famous body language studies at UCLA, found that only about 7 percent of the emotional meaning in a message is composed of the actual words we use. About 38 percent is communicated through the tone of our voice and voice inflection. About 55 percent comes through our nonverbal communication, which includes facial expression, gestures, and posture. This startling statistic reminds us that others believe the visual information that we make available to them before they believe the actual content of the words we use. Even more profound is that all of us believe what we think we see before we believe what the communicator intended to project.

> Nonverbal language is a vital part of the communication process.

Nonverbal language is a vital part of the communication process. Savvy professionals use nonverbal communication as part of the

I can't emphasize enough the importance of congruency between what you say and what you project nonverbally. I've seen a number of professionals whose effectiveness has been undermined because they are perceived as rude, cold, or aloof— often not because of anything they've said but because of the message they're sending through body language. Ironically, nine times out of ten their intention is exactly the opposite. We've found videotaping to be a great tool for fine-tuning this arena as individuals receive direct feedback on what went well and can easily identify any problem areas. In the hospitality business, working at cultivating powerful nonverbal communication helps us to be able to create an even more genuine connection with our guests and clients.

—Kevin Patton, Corporate Training and Development Manager, Manhattan East Suite Hotels

process of connecting with customers and colleagues. They understand that body language that is consistent and congruent with their verbal message builds trust and rapport.

On the other hand, distracting gestures, unconscious movement, and violation of cultural expectations get in the way of the receiver hearing the words and the meaning of the verbal statement. Even the most carefully crafted message will be negated if the speaker's body language and words are incongruent.

Hidden Information

If we rely too heavily on the exact words people speak, we might miss what is actually being said. Using the eyes *and* the ears when communicating gives depth and meaning to a message. How often have you been able to determine what someone is really saying just by reading their facial expression?

The context of the situation often offers a clue, too. Try turning off the volume when watching a movie. Body language and facial expressions provide information about whether the movie is a comedy, a love story, or a horror flick.

Watch a sporting event. You can determine who is rooting for which team by the jerseys, caps, and paraphernalia fans are wearing. You can determine who is a sports enthusiast and who is a casual observer. Energy level, posture, and facial expressions will give you clues as to which team won and which team lost.

Observe people in a restaurant. A group of men and women dressed in suits dining together in the middle of the day may signify a team lunch. A man and a woman having a candlelit dinner, holding hands on a Friday night might indicate a romantic night out. A mom with five kids at a pizza place decorated with balloons might indicate a birthday celebration.

Practice Makes Perfect

We use nonverbal communication unconsciously all the time. But as an intentional, conscious skill, it is the most underrated and least utilized of all business skills. Elevated to a proactive level, it can be a tremendous source of personal power and strength.

There are three steps to projecting energy, confidence, and power.

1. Understand the components of your most effective nonverbal communication.
2. Break the components down and practice impactful, consistent, natural execution. For most people, it begins with eye contact.
3. Adapt the behaviors to your style. It's got to feel authentic and genuine to you before it looks that way to others.

In order to play better golf, you practice your stroke. It takes hours at the driving range practicing the back swing, working on your body position, mastering body movement, and practicing the follow through. Repetition of basic strokes lays the foundation for greater consistency on the course. Continual practice increases accuracy and consistency. Eventually, your brain and muscles respond automatically. You advance to making one entire motion instead of thinking about the individual steps that make up the swing.

> We use nonverbal communication unconsciously all the time. But as an intentional, conscious skill, it is the most underrated and least utilized of all business skills.

In order to deliver better speeches, you wouldn't start practicing by delivering a two-hour monologue in front of one thousand people. You might take a presentation skills class. You would work on content, then you would learn how to use your stance, gestures, projection, and expression to convey your

> Taking charge through the conscious use of nonverbal communication means projecting confidence and competence in any situation.

message. Next, you might deliver one-minute speeches, three-minute experiential stories, and ten-minute tutorials to a group of twenty supportive colleagues.

Gradually, you advance to applying the skills in everyday life. You might lead the next team meeting at the office, introduce the speaker at the sales meeting, or deliver well-crafted presentations to clients and prospects.

In order to project a more impactful presence through nonverbal communication, start by examining your level of competency in the following areas:

- How is your entrance? Are you noticed when you walk into a room?
- Do you offer your hand immediately, regardless of the person's gender?
- Do you make eye contact when greeting people, in meetings, and throughout conversation?
- Are there any distracting gestures that get in the way of people fully connecting with you?
- Are you aware of how you show nervousness under stress?
- Are the nonverbal messages you send clear? Or are people always confused as to where they stand with you?

Taking charge through the conscious use of nonverbal communication means projecting confidence and competence in any situation.

Never Let Them See You Sweat

Skip Kinford, vice president of a large Japanese conglomerate, found himself in a critical business situation that demanded quick thinking and the power of both verbal and nonverbal presence. Skip and two directors from his company were scheduled for a high-level meeting with two directors of their primary customer.

The meeting was strategically planned by the customer to take place in a small conference room at their corporate headquarters at 7:30 A.M. EST, which was 4:30 A.M. for Skip and his team, who had traveled from the West Coast for the meeting. Skip and his team received a published agenda prior to the meeting so that they could accommodate the customer's expectations. When they arrived, the customer turned the tables by announcing the agenda had changed and the meeting would take place in a large conference room. Skip and his team were also informed that now *15* people, including several directors, would be in attendance.

"It became clear pretty quickly that we were being ambushed," said Skip. "In spite of the fact that it appeared we were at a disadvantage, I walked into the conference room, took the chair at the head of the table, stood up, approached the key decision maker, shook hands, and handed him *our* agenda. Agendas were also passed out to the other directors and attendees.

"Without giving anyone else a chance to respond or speak, I again stood at the front of the room and said, 'Thank you all for joining us. We value your time and understand the importance of this meeting. Let's get right to the point.' We won the meeting by respectfully putting the customer back on their heels. We took control of the situation by entering the room with confidence and being proactive in our approach. We controlled the pace and closed the meeting on our terms."

> Our physical presence, posture, handshakes, and eye contact are the first of the body language characteristics that others see. Evaluate your performance in each of these areas. What could you do differently to enhance your presence?

Several dynamics were at play. Between the last-minute changes in the agenda, the change in the size of the meeting room, and the dynamics of fifteen members from the customer team to three members from the vendor team, it would have been very easy to submit to the customer's power plays.

Mr. Kinford's powerful nonverbal communication moved the vendor from a reactive position to a proactive one. By taking the position at the head of the table, standing up, shaking hands with the decision maker, and passing out his agenda, he nonverbally stated, "This is *our* meeting."

Our physical presence, posture, handshakes, and eye contact are the first of the body language characteristics that others see. Evaluate your performance in each of these areas. What could you do differently to enhance your presence?

Energy Is What Makes the World Go Around

Think of people you know who command presence every time they enter a room. What exactly do they do that makes people respond to them? Remember a time when you watched an entertainer's performance. What was it that impressed you? How did he or she command attention? It's a phenomenon that researchers and business professionals continue to study.

Each of us has a field of power. "It is a silent sphere of energy that emanates not only from the mind and physical form but from your heart— which conveys moment by moment, the emotional truth of who you really are, deep down, and what you stand for, care about, and believe."
—Robert Cooper, *Executive EQ: Emotional Intelligence in Leadership and Organizations*

When we ask our seminar participants to describe what physical presence means to them, the most common answers we hear are "energy and confidence." We've all been in a meeting where fellow coworkers are slumped around the table and slouched in their chairs. Even if we weren't tired before the meeting, the low energy from other zapped people is contagious. We feel energized after a workout, pumped up at a sporting event, and enthused at a charity fundraiser. Positive business energy is contagious, too.

The point is, we are made of energy. Professional presence is about exuding it. Each of us has a different style through which energy is communicated. It doesn't have to be hyped-up, extroverted energy. It can be quiet, calm energy, consistent, even-keel energy. As long as it's positive, project it.

Watch an athlete. Even when not performing, their posture, walk, and energy command a room. Such presence comes from constant training, discipline, focus, and personal control. Athletes exude energy and confidence.

A student intern was involved in a research project for a large marketing firm. One of the partners happened to stop by the research library and found the intern slouched in a chair, perusing the massive volumes of data. "And who do we have here?" asked the partner. The intern glanced sideways, then up at the partner as if taking a moment to ponder his response, then looked back down at his book and mumbled, "I'm an intern." Greater presence certainly could have been projected had the young man smiled, stood up, shaken hands with the partner, and introduced himself.

This firm is well known for hiring interns into well-paid, full-time positions. Opportunities to create an impression are fleeting. *When we encounter them, it's up to us to make the most of them.*

What You See Is Not Always What You Get

Appearance is important, too. We tend to make judgments based on the visual data we gather. Dress and grooming are important clues we project each time we encounter someone. Fair or not, perceptions are formed and judgments are made based on this seemingly superficial data. If something is out of context from another's point of view, we may be perceived as odd or ineffective.

Antoinette Jennings is a sales associate for an exclusive department store. She recalls a time when she made a critical error in judgment based solely on appearance. "I was busy with another customer when I noticed a woman walk into our department. She was wearing jeans with holes in them, a funky white T-shirt, and she wasn't wearing any make-up. Typically I try to at least greet people as they come into a department and determine if I can be of assistance. We are on commission, so I hate to miss any opportunities. This time, I admit, I sized her up, thought she couldn't afford our clothes and went back to my customer. I later found out that she selected 12 garments, approached the register and paid for everything with her Platinum American Express card. It was a painful lesson for me, but I will never judge anyone by their appearance again."

> You only have 60 seconds to make a positive first impression.

Likewise, there are times when someone's physical appearance gives us clues that we should believe. Crossing the street when we see a suspicious character who makes us uneasy may keep us out of trouble. It's not always easy to pick up on the exact body language that makes us react. The brain's limbic system is designed to compel us to act on an intuitive level. Sometimes we may not trust someone because of the way they are dressed, or because of the way they make eye contact. Sometimes it's just instinct, a gut reaction, which is important information worth listening to.

Presume, But Never Assume

Pam Grundon, in a past career as a training supervisor, said she learned an invaluable lesson about nonverbal communication. "I gather a lot of information about people and situations based on their nonverbal cues. But once I took action based on an assumption. I assumed that a wrinkled brow, crossed arms, and silence meant that my boss was critical of my ideas, and I made my decision accordingly. It was the wrong assumption. My boss approached me and kindly, but *firmly* said, 'never assume you know what I mean just from my body language. Ask for clarification if you are not certain.' To this day I stop and ask myself, 'Am I making an assumption here?'" Wrinkled brows can mean someone is deep in thought—not negative. Crossed arms can mean someone is defensive and cold—not against an idea. Silence can mean someone is being reflective—not disapproving.

> Nonverbal cues can substitute for, emphasize, or support the verbal message we deliver. Consequently, nonverbal communication strongly influences the way we are perceived.

While it is never safe to assume all information without some questioning, we do gather essential clues about the message someone is trying to deliver from nonverbal communication. The more you study the nuances between others, the better you become at reading people. What we are thinking is typically betrayed through our actions or what is on our face. Nonverbal cues can substitute for, emphasize, or support the verbal message we deliver. Consequently, nonverbal communication strongly influences the way we are perceived.

The reality is that as valuable as nonverbal cues can be in providing us with additional information, we still filter things through our own values and beliefs. One client explains that she often catches herself crossing her arms at networking events because it is a comfortable standing posture for her. She realizes, however, that most people don't see it as such, so she corrects herself when she realizes she is doing it.

You might observe an employee slouching in his chair and not making eye contact during a meeting and assume he isn't paying attention. Experience might support this as a logical conclusion, especially if this individual has a history of being obstinate. But perhaps he just doesn't feel well or is deep in thought. If you assume his intentions are to derail your meeting and you are wrong, you've set both of you up for bitter feelings and a nonproductive work relationship.

Professional presence would demand that he be proactive in handling the situation. He might let you know prior to the meeting that he wasn't feeling well, or explain afterward. In the same respect, before you jump to conclusions about what someone else's motives are, ask them.

The beauty of nonverbal communication is that it gives you information from which to build a conversation. Instead of allowing your assumption to fester and being resentful, you can pull the employee aside after the meeting and say, "John, it looked to me as if you were rather inattentive at the meeting this morning. Are you feeling okay?"

In doing that you've actually done three things: 1) expressed concern for the employee, 2) let him know how his body language appeared to others, and 3) initiated communication to get to the real issue.

The shoulder shrug, slumped posture, a quick wink, rolling of the eyes, crossed arms, and sideways glances can definitely provide clues about what someone is thinking. Gestures provide the perfect opportunity to open the doors for effective communication only if we take the time and have the courage to clarify what we think we are seeing.

> One wise seminar attendee observed, "You don't always get the luxury of being on the receiving end of professional presence, do you? Customers aren't always as gracious and thoughtful as we might expect. It's one of those things you just have to keep dishing out in a positive way, and hope that it gets returned to you, even in small increments."

Mom Was Right

"Stand up straight. Don't drag your feet. If you slouch your spine will permanently shrink and you'll end up two inches shorter." Being told these things when growing up seemed like endless nagging. But those who listened have reaped the rewards.

You don't have to be tall and gorgeous to have presence. Good posture can give the most diminutive of individuals energy and physical

Motivational speaker Peter Lowe explains that "faulty posture is not only the leading cause of back pain, it also contributes greatly to burnout. Bad posture reduces the flow of blood and oxygen to the brain, decreases mental alertness, undermines one's ability to concentrate and even contributes to an attitude of cynicism and gloominess."

"Make an effort, particularly during stressful situations, to keep your posture upright, your shoulders back, your head high, and your muscles relaxed. You should feel buoyant and balanced, with your spine straight and body in alignment. Standing tall will keep you better equipped both physically and mentally to handle stress and prevent burnout."

power. Mom is not the only one with good advice. Experts continue to find evidence that good posture equals not only a stronger presence, but also better health.

Robert Cooper, Ph.D., author of *Executive EQ*, finds that standing or sitting with your shoulders rolled interrupts 30 percent of the oxygen flow to the brain. Studies show that if you take strategic pauses for 15 to 30 seconds every half-hour, you will have increased energy of up to 50 percent and higher productivity of up to 15 percent. It only takes shifting in your chair, correcting your posture, taking a drink of ice water, looking out the window or taking a moment to share a laugh with a colleague to create energy again.

Seated posture is as important as standing posture. Think about how you are perceived when you are seated behind a desk or at a conference room table. The only part of you that is visible is from your torso to the top of your head. You lose more than half of your physical presence.

Evaluate how you sit in your chair. Remember to lean forward when speaking to make a point or when listening to someone else. Enhanced posture can also be achieved by sitting toward the front of the chair as opposed to settling all the way into the seat. Soft chairs and oversized couches do not provide the support that enhances seated presence.

Your mental energy can fuel your muscle presence. When you enter a room, attend a meeting, or conduct any type of business, look and act as if you belong there. Show up ready to be fully present.

Making Physical Contact: The Handshake

Americans are famous around the world for their fast pace of doing business. In parts of Europe and the Middle East, people may sit for hours over a pot of coffee or tea before they even begin to discuss business. In Japan, prospective business associates invest weeks just getting to know one another. Even though they may order a confidential report, a *Koshinjyo*, that gives a detailed account of their potential client, a great deal of time is still invested in developing trust.

> In ancient times, men would grasp forearms in a gesture of peace, and also to check for hidden weapons. As we have become more civilized, we rarely check for personal weapons, so the forearm grasp has become a hand grasp.

Most societies have elaborate rituals for meeting and greeting people, starting with the requirement that you are introduced to a person by someone well known to both parties. Americans move around too much for that and we are in too much of a hurry. It certainly is nice to have a personal connection, but Americans also do a lot of self-introducing.

We also come from many ethnic backgrounds. Each has its ritual, which may include bowing, kissing, hugging, or giving a "high five." But the Anglo-Saxon culture has primarily influenced the greeting ritual in the United States so shake hands.

The handshake is the focal point of the American greeting ritual, and we have evolved important rules surrounding it. Most of the time, the handshake is the only physical contact that we are allowed in a business relationship. We put a lot of emphasis on it. We often allow impressions based on the handshake and the rituals that surround it to determine the future of a business relationship. For better or worse, those first few moments often determine the comfort level and ensuing success of an entire meeting.

Start with the basics. Handshakes actually begin when we make eye contact, before physical contact is made. We can gauge by the look we receive if someone is glad to see us, in a hurry, or not even paying attention to the fact that we are there. Presence is established through friendly, direct eye contact. Once eye contact is made, the hand is extended. Initiating the handshake is the sign of a true professional.

If you wait for someone else to initiate the handshake, you risk being perceived as timid and unsure of yourself. The exception to this is when you are visiting someone else's environment or office. Then it is important that you wait momentarily for them to offer their hand. After all, they are the host. If a handshake is not immediately forthcoming, hold out your hand. Never allow an important meeting to start without a handshake.

A client of ours shared an uncomfortable experience that demanded quick thinking and immediate composure. She extended a handshake to a male client of hers who did not reciprocate the gesture. There she stood, in the middle of the crowded reception area, thinking, "What have I done wrong?" Suddenly, she remembered a conversation with a colleague who previously worked with this client. Being of Hasidic Jewish ancestry, it was not his practice to shake hands with women. She quickly dropped her hand, smiled warmly, gave a verbal greeting, and engaged in conversation.

Next, meet the person's grip web to web and palm to palm and match pressure. If you receive a firm handshake, grip with the same firmness. If you receive a handshake with light pressure, don't squeeze too hard. Cultural differences or health issues may prevent the person from extending a firm handshake.

Shake hands crisply, firmly, with only one squeeze. Mentally do a 1-2-3 count. Then drop. Don't pump up and down more than once. Don't sandwich the other person's hand between both of yours. It suggests that you are trying to overpower, to patronize, or to claim the higher status. Don't bone crush, glad hand, or wimp out with a two-knuckle finger wiggle, the kind of handshake that only includes half of the hand. Save the limp, dead-fish shake for the selected few that need to know that you perceive them as obnoxious, overbearing, or overly impressed with themselves.

When shaking hands, treat men and women with equal respect. From a business etiquette perspective, it is as appropriate for a man to offer his hand to a woman as it is for her to offer first. Gender is not a consideration. The shake should be offered as firmly to a woman as to a man.

Some women are uncomfortable offering their hand to other women. Traditionally, women have either nodded to each other in greeting or hugged one another. But in business, a firm handshake is the appropriate greeting, never the "little lady finger wiggle."

Jason Litton, an investment banker, indicates he gains much of his information about people from their form of greeting. "I was brought up that it was a statement of respect and personal power to always extend a firm handshake. Doing business in today's global economy has taught me differently. The first time I went to Japan, my prospective client bowed. I didn't know what to do, so I clumsily withdrew my hand and bowed back. Now I pay attention to the way people exchange greetings. If it's a firm handshake, I might assume they were taught many of the things I learned growing up. If it's a limp handshake, I try to consider the fact that the person might have arthritis or had been taught to greet others in a different way. If it's a bow, or just a smile, I follow suit. My business experience has taught me to respect the beliefs and practices of others."

> Among friends the shaking of the hand is the most genuine and cordial expression of good-will.
> —Richard A. Wells, *Manners, Culture and Dress*

Jennifer Jacobs, an account executive for a package distribution company, told us she learned an important lesson when confronted with a customer wearing a prosthesis. "I've always been proactive in extending my hand in any business situation. My father taught me I would never be taken seriously if I didn't. Once I was too proactive and ended up being embarrassed instead. I failed to notice my new customer was wearing a prosthesis on his right arm. I quickly extended my right hand, expecting his right hand in return. Instead, he extended his left hand. The smile on my face melted to confusion instantly. Fortunately, my customer was gracious enough to just smile and shake my hand with his left hand. It was a good lesson for me to take a second to assess the information in front of me, then respond accordingly."

However the greeting or handshake is conducted, it should not be rushed. We have so few opportunities to truly connect with individuals in business today. Handshakes are a critical time to establish yourself, your presence, and to be remembered. When shaking hands, hold eye contact until you have determined the color of the person's eyes. Doing so reinforces the connection and helps slow the greeting process down.

The Eyes Have It

The eyes are the windows to the soul. Eye contact is one of the most powerful ways to establish trust and rapport. Effective use of eye contact helps us exhibit confidence as a speaker and respect as a listener.

A professor was rated by his students at the end of the semester. Feedback indicated that the class was not well received. Interviews with the students gleaned responses such as "he's so boring," and "smart guy, great topic, but dull class." Further observation found that the professor's teaching style was to stand behind the podium, read from his notes or present from slides during each class. There was no attempt to engage students in participation or establish a personal connection.

Any speaker can be perceived as boring if he or she is stiff, doesn't make eye contact, is unanimated, or fails to use gestures. Nodding the head, eye contact, and moving toward someone when they speak projects positive reinforcement that you are listening. Body posture and gestures can indicate whether or not we are approachable, receptive, and friendly. Speaking with our back turned or hiding behind a podium or visual aids will fail to build interest.

Like handshakes, the rules of eye contact differ by culture. In the United States, we are taught to make direct eye contact. Eye contact is held while people are speaking as a sign of respect and to demonstrate that we are listening. Some Asian and Middle Eastern countries believe the exact opposite, that eye contact is a show of disrespect. It is important to evaluate under which circumstances to exhibit a specific behavior in order to project the strongest and most appropriate presence for that culture.

> I draw significant conclusions about a person within the first few moments of meeting. A person gains my initial respect by their sense of confidence, posture and dress. I attach trust to the handshake, smile, and eye contact. I anticipate the nature of the working relationship by his or her warmth and openness. Such immediate conclusions are probably not fair—but they are almost always correct.
> —Lee Kricher, Vice President, Linkage Incorporated

It's a Judgment Call

Eighty percent of the decisions we make in business are judgment calls. There is no silver bullet for knowing exactly what to do all the time. The type of appropriate nonverbal communication depends on the situation, the environment, and the audience at any given time. Two things you can count on are:

> Eighty percent of the decisions we make in business are judgment calls. There is no silver bullet for knowing exactly what to do all the time.

1. That you will be perceived as a professional if you have the awareness, intuition, and ability to respond accordingly and respectfully in each business situation.
2. While each component—physical presence, handshakes, and eye contact—is an important entity by itself, the greatest power comes from using them together.

The messages have to be congruent. You can have a great handshake, but if you don't couple it with direct eye contact, you won't be perceived as confident. If you don't enter a room with energy and presence, no one will notice you making eye contact. Heightened awareness, experience, and practice with nonverbal communication will give you added presence in business.

five

Using Space, Territory, and Mirroring and Matching to Make a Connection

In walking with any person you should keep step with military precision, and with ladies and elderly people you should always accommodate your speed to theirs.

—*Manners, Culture and Dress, 1890*

Each of us has a favorite chair at home, a usual parking place at the office, and a typical place where we sit at meetings. We personalize our offices and cubicles with pictures of family, certificates of achievement, and tokens that represent our hobbies. We consider it to be an invasion of space when someone enters our office uninvited or helps himself or herself to something from our desk drawer without permission.

Human beings are territorial by nature. An unwritten protocol exists for every action and interaction from how to meet and greet people to where to sit when visiting someone's office. Understanding and abiding by this protocol is a show of respect to others. It provides the foundation for creating rapport and building trust.

> An unwritten protocol exists for every action and interaction from how to meet and greet people to where to sit when visiting someone's office.

Mi Casa Is Not You Casa

Barbara Jones, a bank manager, resorted to putting her name on her stapler, her tape dispenser, and her pens after constantly having to chase them down after meetings in her office. "I know it sounds so petty," she explains. "But first of all, it makes me look unorganized if I can't find a pen when a customer is opening a new account with us. Secondly, it makes me wonder who's been snooping around my office when I find things missing. It makes me not trust my staff."

> People value their privacy and need to protect and control their personal territory. Studies have demonstrated that if you are talking to someone and inadvertently violate some aspect of his personal space, he may be so upset that he doesn't hear another word you say.
> —Tony Alessandra, Ph.D., *Communicating at Work*

Wendy Herman, an operations manager, said she had an uncomfortable situation with a salesperson selling a communication system. Having researched the product, she scheduled an appointment for the salesperson to do a demonstration. The salesperson arrived at the appointment on time, was dressed professionally, smiled, shook her hand, and then sat down on the corner of her desk. Next he plunked his brief case in the middle of the desk and, while chatting amicably, proceeded to empty the contents of his briefcase onto the client file she had in front of her. Wendy told us, "I was so appalled at how invasive he was that I couldn't even listen to his presentation. The fact that he didn't pick up on how uncomfortable I was offended me even more. Needless to say, we won't be purchasing that particular communication system any time soon."

How Close Is Too Close?

Respect for an individual's space demands awareness of the dynamics in personal and physical proximity. The parameters of personal space differ depending on cultural differences, personal comfort zones, and length of the relationship. Some people are naturally comfortable in close proximity with others. Others claim space by stepping back, leaning away, or looking around the room when space is invaded.

Think about walking into an elevator. When you enter alone, you feel comfortable standing anywhere in the car. When you stop at the next floor, two people join you. What happens? Everybody takes a corner, dividing the space in the elevator equally. More people join you on the next floor. People stand taller, gather their brief cases and packages closer, look at the floor, or stare straight ahead as if deep in thought. Most people are uncomfortable in such close quarters, even with this everyday practice, and work to claim as much personal space as possible.

Jack Presley was attending a customer appreciation event hosted by one of his vendors. As he was standing by the bar waiting for his drink, one of the salespeople from a vendor company caught his eye from across the room, briskly walked in his direction, slung his arm around Jack's shoulder and slapped him on the chest. Overwhelmed by this jovial greeting, Jack offered a stiff smile, a lukewarm hello, and took a step back in an attempt to escape. The salesperson didn't get the hint that he had literally overstepped his bounds.

Social and cultural differences provide the guideline for appropriate space and territory protocol. The safest comfort zone for most individuals is three to six feet. Notice when most people shake hands, they unconsciously lean slightly forward to close the distance and create connection. Some cultures expect and honor even closer proximity like kissing each cheek, hugging as a greeting, and leaning in and talking in hushed tones during a meeting. For other cultures, physical contact and close proximity is considered offensive.

A client of ours told us that she recently received a call from her hair salon to confirm her appointment for the following day. Although she loved the way Nuncio cut and styled her hair, she dreaded his greetings. The Italian stylist showered her with kisses and hugs each time she had an appointment. She told her stylist's assistant that she would be there and then said, "Could you please tell Nuncio not to

A colleague of ours who does team building says, "When I can smell their breath, they're too close!" She carries a can of breath mints with her as a "space claimer." When someone is standing too close, she extends her mints and asks, "Would you like one?" The gesture helps re-establish the appropriate distance between her and the person with whom she is conversing.

kiss me when I see him?" The startled stylist responded, "Oh, goodness, yes, but he won't know what to do!"

Paul Brandt, senior manager for a pharmaceutical company explains, "There is a vice president in our office who used to intimidate me. Some of that intimidation came from his gruff style, but most of it was because he would intrude into my personal space, causing me to back up a step or two. It took me weeks to figure out that he was trying to intimidate me. I got so angry, I decided to fight back.

> Plan ahead for seating arrangements. Whether it's a vendor meeting, staff meeting, a casual or formal meal, or a panel discussion, seating dynamics are critical to its success.

"Armed with my frustration, I prepared for our next interaction. He strode into my personal space, closer than is socially acceptable, and I fought every urge to take a step back. I even took a tiny step forward, which forced him to take a step back. Not only was I charged up with the small but significant victory over my feelings of intimidation, but I've noticed he has treated me with respect ever since. He occasionally tries to crowd my personal space, but for the most part, he takes a step back when I don't budge."

The way we react to and communicate through space and territory is affected by the dynamics of our physical environment and furniture. Take seating arrangements, for example. If you call someone into your office for a meeting and you sit on one side of the desk and they are opposite you, it might be perceived as a power play. The desk acts as a barrier and may hinder open communication. If you sit side by side on the same side of a table or at round table, you create a more collegial atmosphere.

In his book, *Psychiatric Interviewing: The Art of Understanding*, Shawn Christopher Shea, M.D., writes about an exercise used in new clinician training as preparation for seeing patients. "They are given a simple task, to situate themselves so that they feel the most comfortable with regard to conversing with one another. In about 90 percent of the cases, the participants choose a similar position. They sit roughly four to five feet apart. They are turned towards each other, but do not quite directly face one another. Instead, they are turned about a five- to ten-degree angle off the line directly between them, both in the same direction.

"If participants are asked to turn directly toward each other, they complain of feeling significantly less comfortable. The discomfort is related as feeling 'too close.' More specifically, many of the trainees complain that the head-on position forces eye contact, making it difficult to break eye contact without undertaking a significant head movement. This head-on position fosters a sensation of confrontation."

Strategically plan seating arrangements and be consciously aware of body position to gain maximum presence and to create the atmosphere for the message you want to communicate.

Get in Sync

The best skill for building rapport is "matching and mirroring." We build rapport quickly with those who have manners and mannerisms similar to our own. In fact all Homo sapiens have a built-in mechanism to "ape" others' actions. But this has to be done subtly and with intelligence for it to be effective in the business world.

If someone is calm, slow down and stay controlled, with smoother, less emphatic gestures. Show high spirit and enthusiasm when the other person demonstrates it.

A colleague of ours, Carl Boggs, is a straightforward, hard-hitting, bottom-line bank manager. He is traditional in his business manner and is not especially verbal or physically affectionate. When he met Kimberly, a salesperson for a large computer company, she greeted him enthusiastically, pumped his hand, and practically slapped him on the back trying to create instant rapport.

He quickly withdrew. Instead of noting his reaction and responding accordingly, Kimberly moved to fill the awkward silence with nonstop chatter about her company. Within minutes, Carl had decided that Kimberly was not a person he wanted to do business with.

> Many people, particularly business executives, believe a poker face is a strategic advantage. Sometimes it is. But often, you only gain complete credibility with an audience when they feel you're completely open. The viewer generally perceives the warmer, more vulnerable personality as being stronger and less afraid.
>
> —Roger Ailes, Chairman and CEO, Fox News

Mirroring and matching is a phenomenon that occurs on multiple levels of the communication process. It simply means getting in sync with the person or people with whom we are interacting. We do this in both our verbal and nonverbal communication. Mirroring and matching body language helps build trust and rapport. Other important dynamics to consider are matching energy level, facial expressions, tone of voice, vocabulary, and pace.

> Observe behavior first. Then mirror and match back the observed behavior to build rapport and comfort.

A client of ours, Stan Lennox, explained, "At six feet four inches and 250 pounds, I know I stand out in a crowd. I also have a loud, deep voice. Add a dark suit to that combination and I know I can come across as an intimidating force. There are many times in business when my size and my height can be used to my advantage. For example, I always get noticed when entering a room, and I've found that I can be persuasive when certain business situations get to be difficult.

"Certainly though, there are more times when I don't want to intimidate a client or a prospect. I've learned that if I am working with someone who has a more diminutive stature, I try to find a place for us to sit and talk, so I am not towering over the person. I also gauge my height when seated. If I detect the person moving to gain more physical space, I may sit with less erect posture, slow my rate of speech and lower my tone of voice. It all depends what it will take to make the person I am with more comfortable."

The Difference Is in the Details

Page Haviland, Ph.D., a consultant for an international consulting firm states, "You have no credibility if you don't apply mirroring and matching skills to your communication. Mirroring and matching communicates a level of understanding and empathy of that person's world. It is our job as professionals to project that we understand someone's business by tailoring our communication accordingly."

Page explains, "When I was in the Navy I witnessed a man walk into a room full of naval aviators. In an attempt to build rapport and be 'one of them,' he shouted, 'Hey, does that jet you fly have heads up display?' Glancing at each other and rolling their eyes, the naval aviators ignored the man instead of including him in the group. The correct term is '*head* up display,' not '*heads* up display.' It was apparent the man hadn't done his homework. His attempt to bond backfired. He was perceived as a fake and a schmoozer, which consequently affected his credibility with the aviators."

Every business culture has its own terminology. Are salespeople of the company you are prospecting called salespeople, sales representatives, or account executives? Are managers of your new customer's organization called region managers, region service managers, district sales managers, or team leaders? You must work to authentically integrate and incorporate the correct language and its usage so you will be perceived as a viable outside partner as opposed to an uninformed outsider.

Mirroring and matching isn't only used to connect with external customers. It is most effective when incorporated into our everyday personal style. True professionals make the skill a natural part of the communication process to build relationships with everyone they meet and work with.

> One energetic sales manager uses sports analogies in every weekly team meeting. Another corporate executive favors war analogies to communicate business strategies. While such terminology might connect with fellow sports enthusiasts or history buffs, it can also alienate a team member who doesn't share the same enthusiasm for the topic.

A new marketing manager realized he needed a significant budget for the new product he was launching the following year. He realized he had to make some friends in the finance department. Instead of approaching the CEO and saying, "Hey Chuck, I need more money for the Q1 product launch," he put together a business plan, including financial projections and bottom-line results. Then he watched how other managers approached the CEO and evaluated their timing, content, and style.

He presented his request to his boss in his office where the CEO was most comfortable. He made sure the timing was right, he used a professional PowerPoint presentation of graphs and analysis, and he calmly and graciously adapted and mirrored the CEO's nonverbal style. He ended up getting the money because he had done the research, validated the projections, and communicated in nonverbal terms that connected with the CEO.

Follow My Lead

Robin Rice, a property manager for an exclusive hotel company, has learned the power of mirroring and matching. "In a tense situation, irate customers are too emotional to really listen to verbal reasoning. But, on an unconscious level, they do respond to body language. One guest was in the middle of the lobby, screaming at the bell captain. I approached the feuding pair, stepped into the line of fire, so to speak, and angled my shoulders so they were square to the guest's. My immediate objective was to get the disruptive guest out of the lobby. The first break in the tirade I asked the guest his name. He was so startled that I even cared, he replied immediately. In a calm, quiet tone I said, 'Please follow me, Mr. James, and I will take care of this situation for you immediately.'

> Stop your world to connect with others.

"The technique was that as I was speaking, I gestured my arm and hand toward my office door, broke the angle of my shoulders only enough to move my arm and take a step in the direction I wanted us to move. The most important part was that I slightly tilted my head so that I was looking up at him, maintained eye contact as I was speaking and moving so he continued to feel as if I was listening. It worked. He followed me, still ranting and raving, but I was able to get him onto my territory and away from other guests."

Subtle Nuances

Some people use mirroring and matching on an intuitive, subconscious level. Others have taught themselves the subtle nuances to establish rapport. Claire Bowen attended a business lunch with five colleagues. The long, rectangular lunch table was set to accommodate three people on each side, which made it difficult for everyone to make eye contact when someone was speaking. Claire was seated in the middle. She noticed that the people on either side of her had to look around her when sharing conversation and she, in turn, had to look side-to-side during the exchange. She felt as if she were at the sidelines of a tennis match, watching the ball travel back and forth across the net. Without disrupting the conversation, she subtly moved her chair back, which literally opened the line of communication.

Networking events are a classic scenario for observing nonverbal communication and applying mirroring and matching techniques. Picture this. You walk into the meeting room and look for someone you know, or for a place to join into conversation. You observe several groups of people laughing and engaged in hearty conversation. You also see several groups of two people. One group of two is off in a corner, standing with shoulders squared to one another, heads bowed forward, speaking in hushed tones. One pair is standing near the buffet, casually chatting with each other while scanning the room in observation. Which group will you join?

The least threatening group to enter is that larger group of laughing, jovial people. Although it is typically not advisable to join groups of two, the second choice would be to approach the pair that is scanning the room in observation. Their body language indicates openness as the individuals are not standing face to face or making direct eye contact with each other. You would probably not enter the group of two that appear to be in deep conversation as you would, no doubt, be interrupting a confidential discussion.

> The objective of business and social events is to build the relationship with your guests and customers . . . not the food.

A colleague describes a difficult situation where trying to include someone else in conversation turned disastrous. "I am president of an association and was attending our annual national convention. It is difficult to be available to everyone and next to impossible to have an in-depth conversation about anything in this jam-packed environment, but I certainly try to be as attentive as possible.

"A new member wanted to discuss our education programs.

"We were standing facing one another, but I sensed when one of my long-time, treasured colleagues walked up to us. I struggled with staying engaged in conversation with the new member while trying to figure out how to adequately acknowledge my colleague. Finally I just turned from the new member and greeted my colleague with a big hug. She immediately engaged me in conversation and I didn't have time to even introduce the new member.

"It was one of those odd moments in human interaction where you don't quite know what happened, but the new member I was originally speaking to suddenly left the discussion. My colleague and I found her 10 minutes later in the ladies room, crying! We tried to make amends, but she completely shut down and refused to engage in conversation with us. We felt terrible.

The next morning, my colleague and I found her at breakfast and sincerely apologized. She said she had "been ignored" by several people at the convention, which as a new member she didn't find especially encouraging, and then she got the brush-off from the president and her buddy. In her mind, we only confirmed her initial impression that the association was composed of cliquish individuals. The situation apparently kicked up every one of her insecurities.

> Timing is everything, both in verbal and nonverbal statements.

"In retrospect, when my dear friend came over, I should have greeted her but kept my hand literally on the new member's shoulder so she felt connected."

Timing is everything, both in verbal and nonverbal statements. There is an art to joining conversations, making introductions, listening intently, and building relationships all at the same time. One client explains, "When I have to interrupt someone's conversation to acknowledge a newcomer to the group, I gently place my fingertips on the arm or elbow of the person I am speaking with, make eye contact and say, 'Excuse me for interrupting, but I would like you to meet so and so.' Next, I make the introduction and if appropriate, include the newcomer into the conversation, or start a new topic." The key is to not make the first person feel interrupted and to make the new person feel included. It takes some practice. A warm smile, attentive listening posture, good questions, eye contact, and a sincere demeanor are critical to letting people know they are important to you.

six

Taking Charge Through Nonverbal Communication

There is the most delicate shade of difference between civility and intrusiveness, familiarity and common-place, pleasantry and sharpness, the natural and the rude, gaiety and careless-ness; hence the inconveniences of society, and the errors of its members. To define well in conduct these distinctions, is the great art of a man of the world. It is easy to know what to do; the difficulty is to know what to avoid.

—*Manners, Culture and Dress, 1890*

Cori Nickerson, a Seattle salesperson, set out to convince a sea-soned mortgage banker that the title insurance company she represented was worth taking a chance on. Although Cori was young, she had learned to listen intently, to validate information through effective body language, and to keep her answers brief and reassuring.

As the banker described the complex issues and his concerns, he stopped suddenly and said, "Can you handle all of this, Cori? There's a lot of politics involved, a lot of egos, and frankly I'm not sure you have the experience to manage my accounts."

Rather than getting defensive, jumping in and acting overeager, or talking the issues to death, Cori stayed calm and friendly. She looked the older man squarely in the eye, and, after a brief pause, simply said, "No problem. I can handle it."

If Cori had reviewed her excellent credentials or her experience at great length, she would have appeared defensive. Cori knew that the banker was aware of her background, and she *read* that what he was looking for was reassurance. Cori used six simple words, delivered with powerful body language, to give him what he wanted. She created assurance, established presence, and took charge.

The manager or sales professional who wants to be perceived as having power or presence seldom wastes time overexplaining, apologizing, or justifying opinions. Brief, decisive statements delivered with authoritative body language remain one of the most effective ways to gain a desired result.

Up Close and Personal

Doing business in person provides us with a combination of physical, intellectual, and sensory clues. That's why people fly thousands of miles for a one-hour meeting. Otherwise we could just rely solely on teleconferencing or video conferencing. Even when video conferencing becomes as commonplace as e-mail, the impact of being face to face will always be essential to a relationship.

> For maximum effectiveness, we need congruency between our spoken words and our nonverbal language.

We need to hear and see those with whom we do business, and at times, we need them up close and personal. We need to be in their presence to use all our senses to determine whether or not we trust them. We need to shake their hand, look them in the eye, see how they move their body, and check out how comfortable we feel around them.

An individual always has more prestige in person. That's why people wait hours to get tickets to a concert when they already own the CD, or stand in line at the bookstore to meet a well-known author and get an autograph. That's why people brave the weather and the crowds to get a glimpse of the president, the pope, or the latest celebrity. That is why presidents and high-level executives of companies generally stay accessible to their employees. Being able to say you saw, or better yet touched or talked to, a person with power or presence confers a kind of prestige by association. In addition, it is much easier to influence others and exert status in person.

Unspoken Power Plays

In the movie *Shock to the System,* starring Michael Caine, the individual with the perceived power and presence gets his cigar lit. As power shifts back and forth between Michael Caine and his nemesis, they take turns lighting each other's cigar. It became a clear visual signal as to who was in charge.

In the business world, the one with the lesser amount of power does the lighting of the cigar, the pulling out of the chair, the hailing of the cab, and all the other subtle and not-so-subtle things that define the differences between the team member and the leader.

> Dealing professionally with intrusions means that no one ever feels dismissed.

Sending Nonverbal Messages to Colleagues

Feeling empowered and assured on the job includes handling those people who seem to have nothing better to do than to waste your time with too much personal disclosure. One of the most common complaints of both managers and salespeople is the time wasters who stroll in and hang around to chat. How can you minimize the amount of extra time that people spend in your office?

Use a straightforward solution—stand up. If you are seated and busy and someone walks into your workspace and you don't want the interruption, stand up and stay standing. It is difficult for visitors to plop down and feel comfortable if you remain standing. They will generally get to the point and leave. Then you can sit down and get back to work. If they don't get the hint soon enough, you can pick up a file folder and move toward the door.

Dealing professionally with intrusions means that no one ever feels dismissed. Skillfully using less obvious methods means that you don't have to resort to the not-so-subtle glance at your wristwatch, or drumming your fingers on the desk. You are acknowledging the person and giving them your full attention, while not forfeiting your right to end the unwanted interruption.

Telling Lies

It is difficult to give accurate assurances and take charge when we are being lied to about very fundamental issues. Of course, lying occurs millions of times each day in thousands of companies: white lies, corporate lies, guilty lies, jealous lies, lies about why someone was late, or about how we spent the weekend. Sometimes telling a lie can be a kind and considerate act, created to save someone embarrassment or to let someone down carefully. We may use a "soft landing" approach when delivering criticism or bad news, especially if we are the messenger and we don't want to be shot. At other times lies wreak havoc and break trust in both personal and professional relationships.

In a survey of 40,000 Americans, 93 percent admitted to lying regularly at work. Why is candor in business still so rare? Perhaps because, when candor can mean anything from publicly disagreeing with a colleague to delivering bad news to the boss, most people think it means something else: risking your future.

The flip side to telling the truth is being ready to hear the truth: honest opinions can help you make the right decisions.

Playing poker is an extraordinary way to get feedback on how you tell lies and how adept you are at reading other people. Holding a losing hand and pretending you will win the pot requires superb nonverbal skills. You will learn quickly if you are a good liar and also how well you discern when others are lying to you. Being able to size up the other players' body language, detect changes in posture, eye contact, and anxiety levels and ultimately determine if they are telling the truth will help you win in poker. The skills are the same in the business world.

Although it is fairly easy to lie verbally, it is much more difficult to be completely convincing in a falsehood since our nonverbal behavior usually gives us away, and nonverbal evidence is always more believable. When a coworker rolls her eyes, grimaces, and says, "I love the new vacation policy," the obvious message is that she doesn't. When an associate sighs, heaves his shoulders, shoots a dark look, and says, "Of course, I don't mind working late," he would rather not.

There are ten specific signals to look for when you believe someone is not telling you the truth. No single gesture by itself indicates that someone is lying. But if you see several of these together, be wary of the verbal message.

1. There is an incongruency between what is said and how it is said. If someone replies, "No problem, I don't mind if you smoke," in a very low voice while looking pained, the truth is that he or she does mind if you smoke.

2. The person fails to maintain strong eye contact and instead looks at the floor or the ceiling—anywhere but at you.

3. The same information is repeated several times. The repetition is an attempt to make it sound truthful.

4. The voice is higher-pitched and louder than normal. This is an involuntary, often fearful, reaction.

5. The eyes shift, generally to the left. In studying the classic Kennedy-Nixon televised debate, Kennedy's eyes rarely wavered, while Nixon's blinked or shifted constantly. Those who listened on the radio to the debate felt that Nixon was the more credible. Those who watched it on television determined that Kennedy appeared more trustworthy.

6. The pupils of the eyes become smaller. Generally people telling the truth have larger pupils. Tiny pupils are sometimes an involuntary response by the body to a deliberate falsehood.

7. The person swallows harder and more obviously. Again, this is an involuntary physical response.

8. The face is flushed and perspiring.

9. The person speaks at a different rate of speech than normal, generally much faster.

10. A hand is placed in front of the mouth when information is given, in an attempt to muffle the words.

Dealing with a Liar

There are several ways to handle a liar. The direct approach is often best. "Sharon, this sales report seems to be wrong. Federated doesn't buy electronically and your expense report didn't include a trip to New York. Would you help me understand this?" Then watch for any of the 10 signals in her behavior. If her nonverbal signals confirm your suspicions, then, while keeping eye contact, remain silent, maintaining neutral body language, and wait for her response.

If it is clear through nonverbal information that your boss is lying to you, determine the magnitude of the lie and how it directly affects you. Is it just a face-saving device for your supervisor and rather harmless as far as you are concerned? Or are you being compromised and sabotaged?

> Our ability to discern what is really being "said" and where the truth lies is simply our attuned instinct, and generally it will prove to be accurate.

You will feel powerless and victimized if you are genuinely threatened by the lie and elect not to take some action. If your boss says, "Don't worry about your job. Even with this merger, your position is not in jeopardy," but is unable to give you eye contact or any other signs of reassurance, take verbal action. Respond with, "I don't feel that you are being straight with me. What are my chances of surviving the cuts?" will return some control to you.

Our ability to discern what is really being "said" and where the truth lies is simply our attuned instinct, and generally it will prove to be accurate.

Getting to the Truth

If someone has pretended to feel one way while influencing others in the opposite direction, clarification is in order. "Michael, you clearly supported my position on not shipping to delinquent accounts. Now I hear that you don't think our salespeople should worry about whether an account has been paid or not before shipping them more goods. What *is* your position?"

The concern here is that attitudes and private conversations, not verifiable facts, comprise the deceit. But that doesn't mean that clear duplicity should be ignored. As competent professionals, we need to know who is on our side and who isn't and as in all things, this will change from issue to issue.

Once you are clear on the caliber of the lie, you have three options:

1. Sit down and directly confront the liar, carefully reading all signs of body language. If the lie is readily admitted to, graciously close the matter if it is in the best interest of the company. However if it has been broadcasted to the company, damage control on the part of the person who intentionally or unintentionally lied is important. Coming from the source, the clean-up will be much more credible.

2. If you don't know exactly who the liar is, plan a strategy to discreetly find out who may be undermining you. Many times the root of the problem becomes apparent without direct confrontation and no fingers are pointed in the process.

    For example, if you find out that one of your employees has clearly been lying to the vice president about your treatment of your staff, careful questioning of the vice president can reveal who the employee is.

    Watching his or her reaction to a nondefensive question like, "By the way, did you have lunch with Jerry this week?" can confirm suspicions or eliminate possibilities. Then you can follow up with a more straightforward question like, "I feel that I am being undermined by Jerry. Can we discuss it so that all the cards are on the table? Would you tell me exactly what Jerry has told you about personnel issues in my department? I sure don't want any 'us against them' going on."

3. The third option is to try to rise above the lie, to show class and dignity because the lie is unfounded and clearly unbelievable. Unfortunately, if the same lie is told enough times, it begins to have the ring of truth. Although there is a certain amount of complicity assigned to those who don't defend themselves, staying silent is always a choice.

The Power of Silence

One of the things that most of us have learned in business is that it takes much more than the spoken word to convince us. The flip side is that it takes more than the spoken word to get what we want. That is why the appropriate use of silence is an important skill to master.

> When we talk too much, we will eventually give away too much information. But because we live in such a heavily stimulated environment, silence is both unfamiliar and uncomfortable.

When we talk too much, we will eventually give away too much information. But because we live in such a heavily stimulated environment, silence is both unfamiliar and uncomfortable. When we rush in with chatter to fill the void, we can lose control of the encounter.

Al Marchman, a talented attorney and negotiator, delivers appropriately placed silence. He rarely immediately responds to any important question; the pregnant pause gives him a chance to reflect. Often the other person quickly fills up the silence by continuing on, which gives Al unintended but very useful information that he can use effectively.

In the corporate world the person who does all the talking is not necessarily the one with the upper hand. Business transactions prosper when the power of silence is both understood and judiciously used. Making your point forcefully may not be as important as staying quiet long enough to hear what points someone else wants to make. The individual who talks all the time and seldom gives others an opportunity to speak is often resented, and gets a reputation as a blowhard or windbag.

The use of silence to encourage prospective employees to reveal more than they had planned has long been used by the savvy interviewer. However, the most powerful use of silence is in focused listening, neither thinking about what you are going to say next, nor scheming about how you will convince the other person. Focused listening requires mental concentration and physical alertness. Giving someone your undivided attention, acknowledging that person with nods and other nonverbal encouragement, being patient and not interrupting creates an atmosphere of trust. Even if the subject is routine, don't let your mind wander. Work to find some application in your life to what is being said. The better listener in any encounter will end up with more information.

Taking notes can be a silent form of respect in the business world. It also leads to greater accuracy. We need, however, to be careful that we don't look inexperienced by taking voluminous notes in a meeting or appear unable to synthesize complex information.

Soft Power

Claire Olson, a Cleveland business owner, is an example of someone who effectively uses "soft power." "Soft power" is knowing you are in control, but rarely ever having to flaunt it. Influence over others is gained in a less confrontational, more friendly and direct manner.

In board meetings, Claire seldom says much until the meeting is well in progress. What she does, instead, is to keep such focused, positive attention on whoever is talking that most of the participants end up addressing their arguments and concerns to her side of the table.

> Nonverbal communication validates all our verbal information, and it is always more believed that anything we say.

Her well-timed and initially limited verbal communications enable her to influence the direction of the board much better than if she contributed verbose, unfocused chatter. When she does talk, others listen. Her "soft power" approach involves weighing each contribution until she has heard from everyone and then summarizing the best of the contributed information along with her own point of view.

There are many ways to give and receive information. But the most powerful statements come from well thought out information endorsed by supportive, congruent body language. Nonverbal communication validates all our verbal information, and it is always more believed that anything we say.

Step Three

Create Your
Virtual Presence

Electronic Etiquette: Using Both High Tech and High Touch

Think before you speak; pronounce not imperfectly, nor bring out your words too hastily, but orderly and distinctly.

—*Manners, Culture and Dress, 1890*

My God, something just changed," exclaims Michael Lewis in *The New New Thing* in describing Netscape founder Jim Clark. Clark and Netscape have been a major force in commercializing, and thus revolutionizing, e-mail, e-commerce, and all other aspects of the Internet. The speed at which information can be exchanged and the level of efficiency at which business can be conducted have deeply impacted the way we communicate with each other.

> The speed at which information can be exchanged and the level of efficiency at which business can be conducted have deeply impacted the way we communicate with each other.

Out with the Old, in with the New?

Face-to-face meetings have been the basis of business relationships for centuries. Influential world leaders along with hardworking businesspeople still fly thousands of miles each year for in-person meetings. However, the ubiquitous power of technology has put a new face on professional presence. It doesn't take meeting in person to make things happen. Technology has brought global enterprise within the reach not only of large companies, but of one-person e-commerce operations headquartered in an extra room of the house. It has profoundly leveled the playing field.

Has technology smoothed out the bumps in the daily grind or simply given us an unending laundry list of things to do and to learn?
—Marco R. della Cava, journalist for technology, USA Today

Like any new phenomenon, the advances in technology have created a whirlwind of excitement and a push for abandonment of old practices. When Web-based home-delivery grocery services entered the marketplace with a complete list of grocery items and fully prepared gourmet foods, multiple trips to the grocery store and hours in the kitchen were significantly diminished.

Online banking is commonplace. From bill paying to transferring money between accounts to buying and selling stocks, thousands of companies as well as millions of individuals have utilized this convenient and timesaving service.

Palm Pilots have revolutionized calendars and correspondence. In some offices, you are viewed as if you exist in the Stone Age if you use a paper address book.

Voice mail, e-mail, cell phones, Web sites, and e-commerce have become critical components of our business dealings. Each contains significant business risks, because at the heart of communication resides people, not machines, and people are deeply influenced by their feelings and emotions.

For most business professionals, technology has created a whole new way of doing business. In fact, the technologically adept have abandoned most other modes of communication. "Why waste precious time in airports and meetings when business can be conducted efficiently online?" they ask. "Why speak with someone on the phone when e-mail can transfer the information?" they insist.

Those who have not jumped on the technology bandwagon are still resistant to the powerful force of electronic communication and e-business practices. No matter how low tech we may see ourselves, we have to get with the program. *The reality is that most relationships start without the participants seeing a human face.* How we are perceived as professionals often lies strictly in the way we conduct ourselves through electronic modes of communication. Today's relationships either move forward or disappear based on the initial strength or weakness of electronic presence. But no matter how high tech we are, we can't forget that ultimately, we are dealing with a human being.

So, how should business be conducted? Which mode of communication should we use? As business professionals do we rely on high tech or high touch? Opinions vary. Some of our clients state that high tech is the only way to go. It's efficient and convenient. Others are adamant that high touch and dealing with people face-to-face is a critical component to doing business and that high tech has gone too far. Some argue that the efficiency of high tech has impeded the development of human relationships and negatively impacted customer loyalty and retention.

> The human moment is defined as "an authentic psychological encounter that can happen only when two people share the same physical space."

Clearly, there are pros and cons to both high tech and high touch. High tech is the most expedient, cost-effective, and paperless way to initiate contact and to transmit and document information. It is not intrusive, as it gives one the ability to retrieve and respond to messages at one's convenience. High-tech communication enables one to reach the masses quickly and is especially effective across time zones when doing business globally.

Many business professionals will argue, however, that high-tech communication creates an increased possibility for the recipient to misinterpret the intended message. In addition, the sender does not have the advantage of his or her physical presence to communicate the message. The dynamics of facial expression and body language are an important part of effective communication.

Edward M. Hallowell, an instructor of psychiatry at Harvard Medical School, states that a critical component missing in high-tech communication is what he describes as *the human moment*. The human moment is defined as "an authentic psychological encounter that can happen only when two people share the same physical space." Dr. Hallowell explains that "the human moment has two prerequisites: people's physical presence and intellectual attention."

That explains much of the emotional frustration experienced by business professionals. Face-time, human moments, and good, old-fashioned workplace camaraderie are diminishing. Businesspeople have so much on their minds, they often forget to take a moment to say "hello" to colleagues and direct reports when they arrive at the office, they may no longer pay attention to birthdays and important family issues, or they may fail to take the time to acknowledge accomplishments or concerns.

As consultants to companies nationwide, we hear repeated accounts of incomplete communication and examples of feeling isolated and confused in the workplace.

"My boss is always out of town, and when he's in the office we never seem to have time to go over important issues. It's hard to stay on track with what he's thinking and how I can best support him."

"I just completed a huge project for my manager, which took me months to research and prepare, and she e-mailed me a 'thank-you.' She didn't even take time to stop by my office."

"I just received a fabulous promotion and the responsibility of managing a new million-dollar client account, but I can't get enough information from my internal resources that I need to move it forward. E-mails just don't provide all the context I require to understand how to handle these new customers."

We've all been there. In some way, shape, or form, we've experienced the doubt, confusion, or alienation that stem from high-tech communication or the lack of interpersonal communication. A client of ours explains, "I promised my customer an e-mail document that included a summary and next steps resulting from a meeting. After I e-mailed it to her, I followed up with a voice mail to let her know that the document had been sent and that I just wanted to make sure she received it. Two weeks went by without a word from her. I know people are busy and I know she had other important issues to deal with. But e-mail and voice mail that aren't responded to create stress and mental anguish that could be diminished with a quick reply."

> Human contact and personal connection are vital to our well-being and productivity.

Human contact and personal connection are vital to our well-being and productivity. Recent studies at Carnegie Mellon University examined how people were affected by spending time online. They found higher levels of depression and loneliness in people who spent too much time connected to the Internet. Additional studies suggested that the electronic world, while useful in many respects, is not an adequate substitute for human contact.

The Best of Both Worlds

How do we establish an effective electronic presence and find the balance between high-tech and high-touch practices?

Companies can balance high tech and high touch by focusing on and implementing e-care management systems that add value to the customer by combining high tech with high touch. A publication of *Managing the Impact of Technology on Sales and Marketing* (vol. 1, no. 3), released by IMT Strategies in Stamford, Connecticut, reports that, "To build stronger customer relationships, organizations need to increase their investments in programs that hard-wire their customer operations, analytics and supporting data flows and find new, interactive approaches to building customer loyalty."

Amazon.com has mastered the melding of high tech and high touch. As a company of avid readers, the Professional Image, Inc., has become a loyal customer of Amazon.com. Although we still enjoy the high-touch experience of perusing the shelves in a bookstore and curling up with a cup of coffee in one of the store's comfortable chairs, busy schedules don't always permit such a luxury. Nothing beats the efficiency of Amazon's technology in finding the book or resource we are looking for, even if we don't know the entire title

Scientists have determined that positive human-to-human contact reduces the blood levels of the stress hormones epinephrine, norepinephrine, and cortisol. Nature also equips us with hormones that promote trust and bonding: oxytocin and vasopressin. The levels of these hormones rise when we feel empathy for another person—in particular, when we are meeting someone face to face. Furthermore, scientists hypothesize that in-person contact stimulates two important neurotransmitters: dopamine, which enhances attention and pleasure, and serotonin, which reduces fear and worry.

—*Harvard Business Review*, January-February MCMXCIX

or the author. Amazon.com is user-friendly and responsive. Customer service has been built into the technology.

Within minutes of the customer placing an order, Amazon.com acknowledges receipt. The customer is assured that the order was not only received, but that action is being taken. A detailed report reflects the content and timing of the order to be shipped. If something is backordered, an estimated ship date is quoted. A proven track record of consistent communication and effective technological systems has created loyal customers.

> Combining the most effective components of high tech and high touch allows companies to conduct business quickly and cost effectively while connecting people, building rapport, creating an emotional bond, and building business relationships.

But it doesn't stop there. Additional perks enhance the experience of the human moment even when driven by technology. Books arrive with bookmarks; large orders arrive with other promotional items such as mouse pads. Unsolicited acknowledgments of appreciation just "show up." After we had placed an order of five books, we received a travel coffee cup, separate from the order, just as a gift of appreciation. Some dollar amounts elicit an e-mail gift certificate to be used with the next order. Marketing ventures? Sure. Effective in building customer loyalty? Absolutely.

It's like the feeling you get upon receiving a personally written thank-you note or finding a birthday card in the mail instead of bills or junk mail. It's a nice surprise. It's refreshing. Combining the most effective components of high tech and high touch allows companies to conduct business quickly and cost effectively while connecting people, building rapport, creating an emotional bond, and building business relationships.

As professionals we can balance high tech and high touch by creating the same kind of consistency and systems though our virtual presence. Many of our clients send a brief informational e-mail to customers each month. The intent is to offer new ideas and creative business approaches, as well as to keep in touch. Another client whose business is conducted over the Internet makes it a point to visit customers in person at least twice a year. If locations are too remote, a personal follow-up phone call is initiated instead of making a visit.

Simple gestures such as a handwritten note, an invitation to breakfast or lunch, or a quick telephone conversation are other ways to add the human moment component to the intensity of business conducted through technology. The trick is to strategically determine how customers, clients, and colleagues can be made to feel the human connection even through cyberspace. Consistency in communication leaves individuals feeling that personal needs have been met.

> When people and the inherent misunderstandings that go with human communication are involved, there can be no "etiquette-free" zone.

High tech or high touch? How do you determine the best way to communicate your message? The answer is to use both. Electronic etiquette saves relationships and businesses from critical misunderstandings. It provides common ground rules so everyone can easily function on the same playing field. When people and the inherent misunderstandings that go with human communication are involved, there can be no "etiquette-free" zone. Granted, as technology changes, the rules will change, too. But guidance and common practices can facilitate effective communication.

Consider the Following E-Etiquette Guidelines:

1. Evaluate the content of your message. Determine which mode of communication will create the most effective delivery of your message. There are times when you must make a judgment call to determine if a live telephone conversation or an in-person visit will make a greater impact than using voice mail or e-mail.

2. Keep in mind that everything you send is a reflection of you and your professionalism. Misspelled words, incorrect grammar, and an abrupt personal style will hinder communication and negatively affect the way you are perceived as a business professional. While voice mail, e-mail and other written correspondence are critical to business communication, they can be one-sided.

3. Stage the scenario and create the environment that will be most conducive to open communication. The high-touch approach, such as in-person meetings, dining with a client or colleague, or attending an event together provide the opportunity to read nonverbal cues and pick up on dynamics of

personal style that are often not visible in electronic communication. In addition, people disclose more information in person once rapport has been built.

4. Evaluate your personal style and the effect it will have on each receiver of information. For example, snapping out a message, via e-mail or voice mail, stating, "I need those reports by 3:00 P.M.," could come across to some as an efficient reminder. Others may perceive the message to be demanding and inconsiderate. Incorporating the human component by giving the message a softer landing could help you in getting what you want while still being considerate of others. This statement might be more effective, depending on the style of the receiver: "I know you have a lot on your plate right now. We agreed that the reports you are generating for the team meeting would be ready by 3:00 P.M. today. Please let me know if there is anything I can do to help so I can have them by then."

5. Ask each person with whom you communicate how they like to receive information. Travel schedules, time zone differences, and personal preference are just a few of the components that determine how individuals best "hear" information. It's never safe to assume that because you e-mailed information in the last communication, that voice mail, a conference call, or video conferencing would be a better choice for the receiver the next time. It is always best to ask the question, "How would you like to receive this information?" It's also important to determine expectations and next steps in the communication process.

> We call things we don't understand complex, but that means we haven't found a good way of thinking about them.
>
> —Tsutomu Shimonura

Determining whether to use high tech or high touch to create your virtual presence is a judgment call. The most effective approach is to use the appropriate mode of communication based on the situation. This chapter sets the stage for considering both approaches to communication. Chapters 8 and 9 provide you with specific e-etiquette regarding the use of the telephone, voice mail, cell phones, pagers, and e-mail. The combination of the three chapters gives you guidelines for creating a powerful virtual professional presence.

eight

Phone Presence: Office, Cell, Conference, and Voice Mail

Be not tedious in discourse, make not many digressions, nor repeat often the same matter of discourse.

—*Manners, Culture and Dress, 1890*

In the television game show, "Who Wants to Be a Millionaire?" host Regis Philbin asks a contestant a series of questions, each with an incrementally higher price tag. On the road to one million dollars, the contestant has three "lifelines" for help should he or she "get stuck." One of the options is the phone call. He or she is permitted to make one telephone call to the person of choice who will presumably know the answer to the pending question.

Prosper or Perish

The telephone is a lifeline. We would be lost without the telephone in business. Certainly business could never get conducted as quickly and efficiently without it. When used correctly it is an excellent tool for sharing information, and staying in touch. But have we become so dependent on electronic modes of communication that we've substituted telephone and voice mail conversations for face-to-face conversations and human connection?

Sterling Nelson, a practicing psychologist, believes that we have created a psychological dependence on electronic means of communication. Observe daily behavior: Telephone communication is visible everywhere we are. We have a telephone in our office and in several rooms in our home. Cell phones are used in the car, the elevator, the movie theater, your favorite restaurant, the grocery store, golf course, and even at weddings, funerals, bar and bat mitzvahs. Many of us have developed an intense need to be connected and stay available at all times. With the "everything has to be done yesterday" phenomenon, we've put ourselves on call 24/7.

> Many of us have developed an intense need to be connected and stay available at all times. With the "everything has to be done yesterday" phenomenon, we've put ourselves on call 24/7.

How do you maintain and project consistent, positive professional presence whether you are answering the telephone in your home office at seven o'clock in the morning, on a lunchtime conference call with clients, or in a busy airport at ten o'clock at night?

Think About It

"Stop, Look, Listen, and Evaluate." The guidelines the crossing guard taught us as we walked to school still prevail with an added step. Whether you are at your desk, at the office, riding the train, or on the street, stop, look, listen, and evaluate before you answer the phone. Where are you? Is it an appropriate environment to answer the phone? Will you be able to confidently and professionally express yourself in your present environment?

One of our clients was driving a customer to the airport. She was expecting a call from her assistant regarding the customer's rescheduled flight, so when her cell phone rang, she answered it. Her husband was on the line, with details of the romantic get-away weekend he had planned. She was listening with delighted attention when she realized the volume was so loud, that her customer could overhear a good part of the conversation. Instead of acknowledging his initiative with praise and excitement, she could only weakly reply to her husband, "Ah, I'm with a customer at the moment, can I call you back later?" Our client found herself in an embarrassing predicament with both her customer and her husband.

It's Not a Management Tool

A former vice president of sales for UPS Worldwide states that while voice mail is an excellent tool for communicating information or giving colleagues or employees a heads up on something, it can be a tool that is misused. Leaving a message like 'We probably need to discuss the proposal before tomorrow's meeting. Please call me today after 3:00 P.M." conveys the importance of the message, but doesn't tie up someone's time with rambling verbiage that may contain confidential information.

Voice mail is not a foolproof communications vehicle. "It seems as though many people try to manage via voice mail," says our client. "They think just leaving a voice mail for someone completely removes the sending party from any more responsibility for the issue at hand. A manager might leave a voice mail to his sales team and say, 'I need those reports' and that would be the end of it. There is no feedback, no clarification, and no conversation to determine if the person understood what is being requested of him or her and when it is due. In the same respect, a subordinate might leave a message for a direct supervisor and say, 'We have a problem,' state the problem, and fail to follow up. Suddenly the problem would become my problem and he or she would just assume it would be taken care of."

> Voice mail could state the issue, but only an in-person meeting would solve it.

This game of "monkey, monkey, who's got the monkey" was a way to transfer accountability, or the "monkey," but not in a consensual manner. I used to have a sign in my office, 'No Monkey Leaving.' Unfortunately, voice mail can be used as a scapegoat. How many times have you heard, 'Well, I left it on your voice mail'?

"I made it a practice that major problems or significant decisions were not to be solved with voice mail. Voice mail could state the issue, but only an in-person meeting would solve it. I would have my team member come to my office with the issue and a possible solution. I would give advice, help problem solve, provide support and resources, but it was important to keep the accountability where it belonged."

> Only 30 percent of phone calls placed are completed. So 70 percent of the time, we are either hanging up or leaving a voice mail.

Give careful thought in determining which vehicle is most appropriate for the information you need to communicate. Voice mail should not be used as a substitute for face-to-face communication. Difficult issues, confidential discussions, and lengthy problem-solving strategies should be conducted in person, not over the phone or via voice mail. However, voice mail is an excellent means of framing the issues and providing background information.

Guidelines for Your Voice Mail Greeting

1. Your outgoing message should be given in a friendly voice, stating your name, and requesting that the caller leave a message and phone number. Keep it brief and to the point. Callers don't want to spend the time listening to where you may be or how sorry you are that you missed their call.

2. Avoid being cute or flippant. While talking like Daffy Duck, Ross Perot, or Barry White may be funny at home, it doesn't convey the credible first impression that most of us want to communicate. Even at home, callers receiving a very humorous message are charmed the first time and even the second time; after that it can cease to be humorous and begin to get irritating.

3. If you choose to keep the same voice mail message and not modify it daily, it should still be changed—like the oil in your car—every three months.

4. If you make your daily status available to callers, it demonstrates excellent presence, but it also takes a significant commitment. Every evening or early morning requires an update no matter where you are or how you feel. If you are really ill, have an assistant or colleague leave the updated announcement.

When callers hear a message on your line that is dated a week ago or even two days ago, you lose credibility.

5. Occasionally call your own number to evaluate how you would be perceived by a new customer, colleague or vendor.

Guidelines for Leaving Voice Mail Messages

1. Keep three by five cards next to the phone to jot down your main points prior to making a phone call. If you reach your caller in person, you will be able to remember all your important issues. If you get voice mail, you will be equally prepared.

2. Always identify yourself by leaving your name and your company name. Don't assume that your voice will automatically be recognized.

3. Keep voice mails friendly, short, and clear, with an indication of next steps or action required.

4. If the voice mail is lengthy, leave your phone number clearly and distinctly at the beginning and the end of the message.

5. If the voice mail is lengthy, you may want to give the recipient a heads-up indicating that you have gone into some depth and he or she may want to review it at a more convenient time.

6. For lengthy voice mails, you may want to consider abbreviating them so that they are not deleted or ignored by the recipients.

> A colleague of ours stated, "As soon as I detect someone is going to leave a long, rambling message and I'll get a sore ear, I hit '* 3 for Delete.'"

7. Consider, too, the number and the length of the messages you leave times the total number that the recipients may receive in a day. Listening to one or two hours worth of voice mail a day is a burden, especially if someone is calling long distance to retrieve messages.

8. If the option is available, review your voice mail before sending it. You can coach yourself on improved voice quality, friendliness, and succinctness. Most systems will allow you to erase it and start over if you don't like what you said or how you said it.

9. Never leave a harsh or negative voice mail. As a one-way assault, it doesn't facilitate communication. It can be listened

to over and over, forwarded, archived, and put on a speaker-phone to share with the office. You may even have a conciliatory conversation prior to the recipient retrieving the negative message. Then when the unplayed negative message is retrieved later, it starts the bad feelings all over again.

10. Due to the non-secured aspect of voice mail, confidential information is best shared in person.

11. Don't leave voice mails where background noise from loud restaurants, jammed bars, clamorous parties, or boisterous family gatherings can be heard.

12. Return all voice mail the same day, even if you end up leaving a voice mail, too.

13. Be sure to check your voice mail at least twice a day and more if you receive time-sensitive information. If you will not be checking voice mail for a period of time, be sure to indicate that on your outgoing message and leave a date when you will be retrieving and responding to voice mail.

14. Compliments or encouragement are one of the most welcome messages to hear. No one ever resents a kind word. Surrounded by directives and demands, a sincere, succinct kudo is a welcome oasis.

15. Start on a human level with a brief, sincere greeting and end on a human level with another short but authentic expression of regard, concern, or good wishes.

One client returned a call to a customer at 9:00 P.M., and when the customer actually answered the telephone, she was so rattled that she sputtered, "Oh! I wanted your voice mail!" and hung up.

The Live Voice on the Phone

Since we started with how phone communication works 70 percent of the time—without a two-way conversation—we now need to address the other 30 percent of the time. The most effective way to establish telephone presence is to actually *answer* the phone live.

Start by smiling. Even without a video image, smiling is seen and experienced over the phone. Smiling affects the quality of your voice. You sound bright, friendly, and enthusiastic.

To create more energy, stand up while talking on the phone. The exception would be if you were in a car, of course. If you are interested in documenting exactly how your voice changes based on your body position, call a voice mail system that allows you to review and erase your message. Then leave the identical message using three different positions: First, seated in your chair; then, leaning over and throwing something away in your wastepaper basket; and finally, standing up with your diaphragm expanded and your energy maximized.

> To create more energy, stand up while talking on the phone. The exception would be if you were in a car, of course.

Now that you've learned how to maximize your voice quality, here are tips from A to Z.

Phone Tips from A to Z

A. Make telephone appointments for important calls when you need to discuss matters in depth, just as you would make person-to-person appointments. Being on someone's calendar at 3:00 P.M. on Tuesday will give you, your phone call, and your information almost the same level of importance as an in-person meeting.

B. Never leave your phone number when the person you are calling doesn't know you and has no idea why you called. You may never receive a phone call back, and that puts you at a disadvantage when you call again.

   However, do leave your name and a brief message either on voice mail or with a receptionist or secretary. Even without leaving your phone number, you can start building the relationship.

C. Don't be offended if the secretary asks, "Will he or she know what this is regarding?" The question may sound condescending, but busy managers and executives receive scores of calls a day and often need a memory jog.

D. When calling medium-to-large corporations, always identify yourself and your company, even if you have called many times before. If you have a distinctive voice or accent that is easily recognized, you may get someone who doesn't know you and get off to a bad start if you are mistaken for someone else.

E. If you call small firms regularly, judge when it is time to drop your company name and just give your first and last name. When you build rapport and establish a relationship with the individual answering the phone you typically recognize each other's voice. It is a show of respect to identify yourself if you hear an unfamiliar voice.

F. If you are repeating the same information on the phone that you have said many times before, take a tip from professional speakers who often say the same thing two hundred times a year, and make sure it is fresh. It may sound stale to you, but don't let it sound jaded by turning it into monotone mush.

G. Never get irritated with an assistant because the boss is consistently unable to take your phone call. If you lose your presence with the secretary, you probably will get a bad review when your message is passed on. That is why they are called gatekeepers. Stay on their good side.

H. If your calls are not being taken, ask when the best time is to return calls, but don't whine about it.

I. Your voice will sound happier, your manner will be more relaxed, and your presence will increase when you concentrate phone work on Thursdays and Fridays. People are much more receptive to phone calls closer to the weekend.

J. Don't say, "How are you today?" unless you know the person you have called and genuinely care how they are. Otherwise, you will be immediately written off as another telephone solicitor.

K. Review your bullets of information so that you are certain to cover all important points.

L. It is always easier to say "no" over the phone than in person. If the decision is important, request a meeting because we are always more powerful in person. If what you hear isn't what you expected, you will be able to negotiate better in person for your Plan B.

M. Even though you have introduced yourself to the receptionist, reintroduce yourself to the person you are calling so that there are no mix-ups.

N. Don't call clients by their first name on the phone until a relationship has been established.

O. Don't say, "Is this a good time to call?" when phoning someone you don't know. You will sound weak and wishy-washy, and it is never a good time to talk to someone you don't know. However, it is considerate when both parties are well acquainted and the conversation will take more than 15 minutes.

P. When you do know the person well, and the phone conversation is certain to be lengthy, offer the courtesy of scheduling a phone meeting at a later time. You will both be better prepared.

Q. "Call waiting" is one method for a single-person firm to do business economically. When people work out of their homes, "call waiting" is a common option. But if you initiated the call to a client, think twice about putting that client on hold while you take another call. If you do, then be up front and say, "May I put you on hold just a brief moment? I am the only person here right now." Then wait for an answer. Don't put someone on hold more than once. Otherwise you will stretch the boundaries of his or her patience and the elasticity of goodwill. There is a certain amount of inference that the unknown caller is more important than they are.

R. If you have your calls screened so that a caller has been announced to you, or their name appears on your Caller I.D. recognize the caller immediately with, "David, this is Margarita. Good morning." Don't pick up the phone with, "Margarita Porto, here." It is an impersonal way to greet someone when you are supposed to know his or her name.

S. If your calls go directly to you or a voice mail system, answer your phone with your name: "David Smith" or "Good morning, this is Smith." If you are answering the phone at someone else's desk, answer with, "This is David Smith's desk."

T. Return all calls the same day or have someone at your office follow up.

U. If you call someone and are disconnected, you are responsible for redialing, even if they accidentally hang up. Since you placed the call, you know how to reach them.

V. If someone walks into your office while you are on the phone, motion him or her out the door or into a seat, but don't interrupt your phone conversation.

W. When you mistakenly take a phone call that you are not prepared for, spend a few minutes on the phone as a courtesy and then reschedule it at a later date. You will lose credibility when you aren't prepared.

X. If a client or coworker is, for legitimate reasons, extremely angry on the phone, quietly listen without interjecting anything. Then, using tact and diplomacy, state your case. If you end up going in circles, suggest you need more information and then set up a phone meeting. If anger disintegrates into rudeness or abusiveness, don't respond. Just calmly say, "For the moment, I don't think we have all the facts to resolve this. I will call you tomorrow after I have done more research." End of conversation.

Y. Before ending the conversation, summarize the call to make sure each of you has the same understanding, and determine next steps.

Z. Even if you are in a rush, say good-bye, but then wait for it to be reciprocated. Otherwise, it feels like you have hung up on the person to whom you were speaking.

Speakerphones, Not Loudspeakers

Conference calls are an excellent mechanism for holding a meeting for several individuals in two different locations. But conference calls require the use of a speakerphone and speakerphones typically have to be loud so that all parties can hear one another. We recommend the following protocol for establishing and maintaining presence for conference calls and using speakerphones:

1. Hold the conference call in an office or conference room where the door can be closed and no one will barge into the room. Speakerphones amplify voices. There may be parts of the meeting or conversation that you don't want overheard. Confidential calls should be made in privacy and should not be broadcasted.

2. Appoint one person to initiate the call. This person is responsible for linking all callers at the designated meeting time. When everyone is present, make introductions and greetings so everyone is acknowledged.

3. It is not always easy to recognize and remember voices, so identify yourself when you join a conversation, when you speak and when you leave the conversation.

4. Speak clearly and project your voice. It shows consideration to ask the person if they can hear you well enough.

5. If you begin a conversation on the telephone and then include others on the call, ask permission or immediately announce that you are putting the call on speaker. Be certain to let the person on the line know who is in the room with you. "Larry, I have Alex Henderson and Joey Clifton with me." Alex and Joey should then greet Larry.

Caveats for Cell Phones

Our seminar groups consistently report that their number one pet peeve for cell phone use is having to listen to someone's personal conversation when riding

As senior managers in their organization, Jill Smelter and Joe Serrino were sitting in their boss's office. Their boss, the CFO, was playing his messages on speakerphone and the group was half listening and half talking. But when the CEO's voice was heard, they all stopped talking and listened. The CEO covered several issues and then ended with, "And Harry, we really need to 'can' Joe Serrino. He's not the right person for the job. You decide how you want to handle it." The entire group was in shock. The CFO quickly realized what a blunder he had made playing his messages over speakerphone. He offered an immediate apology. Joe stood up, nodded to his boss and numbly left the room.

A client of ours attended an Elton John concert. To her dismay the person in front of her continuously stood up and alternated between holding her cell phone in the air and talking on it. The woman would shout into the phone, "Listen, remember where we were when we first heard this song?" then, "Isn't he great?" and "Can you hear that?" The man behind her shouted, "Hey, we all paid for our tickets. Put that phone away."

the train, sitting on the airplane, or in other close public quarters. The second-most mentioned frustration is hearing a cell phone ring in a public place, including meetings, movie theaters, or restaurants. Used in private, cell phones facilitate conversation and save time. Overuse in public is inconsiderate and causes disruption.

Cell phone protocol asks for these considerations:

1. Consider whether or not it is an appropriate time to make a call.
2. Consider where you are and who may overhear the content of your conversation.
3. Excuse yourself and make the call in private if the timing is appropriate.
4. Speak clearly. If you have a bad connection and are breaking up tell the person you will call him or her back.
5. Keep cell phones turned off in meetings and quiet settings.
6. Keep personal business to a minimum, especially if you are using a cell phone that is paid for by the company.
7. When in the company of others, ask permission to take the call.
8. Do not transact important business matters on the phone if you are in the presence of others who are not part of the transaction.
9. If you use the cell phone when driving, use an earpiece or have a speaker installed so your calls are hands-free for safety.

Building Virtual Relationships

Many effective and lasting business relationships have been established over the telephone. Others have ended before they begun.

Greer T. is an outside contractor whom one of our custom video production clients used for voice-over work. She destroyed a very important relationship due to her significant indiscretion, lack of professionalism, and a failed application of technology.

As a voice-over talent in L.A., she called the producer of a project in his office in Dallas and left him a short, reasonable voice mail. Then she clicked the disconnect button on her phone and placed another call. The problem was that her phone read that as "conferencing" and the entire phone call placed to her girlfriend was recorded on his voice mail. The conversation severely criticized and disparaged the producer with references to his "big butt and no brains." Greer had never met the producer in person so her comments were particularly off-base. So when she inferred to her girlfriend that her source of information was our client, it made it doubly bad.

> Many effective and lasting business relationships have been established over the telephone. Others have ended before they begun.

When the producer called our client and played back the voice mail from Greer, she was in shock. Embarrassed and humiliated, she immediately apologized and indicated that she would call Greer and conference all three of them together.

When Greer answered the phone, our client explained the situation with clenched teeth and a calm but forced manner. The first words out of Greer's mouth were, "Oh —" During the three-way conference call the emotional intensity only got worse and the producer and Greer ended up yelling at each other. Today our client says, "Even two years later, I still don't contract with Greer, no matter how talented she is, because the professional trust is broken and she handled the damage control so badly. In addition to losing a real talent with Greer, I still can't get the producer to return my calls."

Then the other side of the coin is Teresa Lee, a customer relations' manager who exhibits excellent people skills. Teresa explains, "Ninety percent of the business I do is conducted over the telephone. I want my clients to perceive me as dependable, proactive, and helpful. It's important to consistently project this message through my phone work and voice mail messages.

"In times of frustration, I watch what I say to my client on the phone and to my coworkers afterward. There is no value to expressing every feeling, every frustration. Sometimes we just have to swallow our disappointment and wait for another opportunity."

Three principles form the foundation for a sound telephone business relationship:

1. *Genuine caring.* People are more apt to respond to you if they know you have their best interests at heart and you demonstrate a willingness to do whatever it takes to make sure their business needs are met. Always take time to connect on a personal level by finding common interests or offering non-business information that might be helpful. You don't have to spend a lot of time doing it, just enough so that the relationship is first and the business transaction is second.

2. *Respect for people and expressing an appreciation for their time and contribution.* If the person is busy, arrange for a time to call back. You will never get enough mind-share to complete the business at hand if a more pressing matter is distracting them. Showing courtesy is more than just saying "thank you," it is demonstrating your concern for their schedule and their immediate, pressing issues.

3. *Being focused and prepared for the telephone call and the business at hand.* Have a list of items on a three by five card that you need to cover in the phone conversation, while being sure to encourage a discussion of their thoughts and needs as well.

nine

The Use and Abuse of E-Mail: How to Get the Best from It

Let your discourse with men of business be short and comprehensive.

—*Manners, Culture and Dress, 1890*

E-mail communication allows us to be responsive and accessible. It is more convenient than face-to-face contact because it can be written and retrieved at our convenience. We can forward it, reply with one click, or send it to a list of a hundred people by hitting one button. We can literally "talk" to others worldwide in a matter of seconds. It is the most significant communication tool that we have to bring people in many locations together to share information, easily and economically.

Steve Case, founder of AOL, answered his own e-mail for years . . . until the volume of his daily e-mails topped 5,500.

A Medium for Both Career-Limiting and Career-Advancing Moves

While e-mail technology is extremely cost-efficient and has the capability to make us more productive, it has also created its own set of problems. E-mail cannot be considered an "etiquette-free" zone and used recklessly and without concern for the damage it can do.

Individuals have ruined personal and professional relationships by sending blunt, critical, and error-filled statements via e-mail.

People say things through electronic correspondence that they would never say to someone in person. Feeling anonymous and unaccountable, they broadcast e-mails that get everyone's attention in the short term, but create much larger problems in the long term. Discernment in its use becomes a mandate.

With all its fantastic properties, e-mail also doesn't provide the human context that is often required in order to be clear on intent or meaning. No single communication tool can function alone to the exclusion of others and meet all the dimensions that a professional relationship requires.

CC: or CYA?

Every time we cc: or broadcast one of our own e-mails, we are making a statement about ourselves and creating an impression in the mind of the receiver. If the content is positive, affirming, or ideally moving business forward, that's one thing. But often it is either unnecessary information to forward to others or just plain divisive.

> Do you feel more like an e-mail address than a human being? We have to be seen by another's eyes in the world to be real.
> —Robert Cooper, *Executive EQ: Emotional Intelligence in Leadership and Organizations*

For example, if the e-mail dialogue has been between peers and the originator decides to also cc: his or her boss, it's a power play. It says that the same degree of attention won't be paid unless someone in a higher position reviews it. It infers a lack of trust. There is also the implied message that if the e-mail is broadcasted to enough people, the responsibility is now diluted and it's not the sender's responsibility anymore.

E-mail doesn't provide the context of body language. Facial expressions and voice cues are missing in the process. It's often a one-way communication with not enough back-and-forth discussion to clarify issues. The mistaken notion is that once an e-mail has been sent, a conversation has taken place. But it's not a real conversation because the give and take is delayed and limited to text on a screen. However there are occasions when that reflective period can be useful.

The Absence of Subtleties

Complex and subtle business cultures and protocols that are obvious in live meetings are often not obvious to someone alone at night in a den or hotel room at his or her keyboard. The absence of normal social restraints can create loose cannon communication.

The amount of time it takes to do damage control on one angry e-mail that was widely broadcasted with too many exclamation points, half-truths, or inaccurate information is significant. On the part of the original, intended recipient, it takes cooling off. Then it requires assessing the damage, getting the correct information, composing a response that is balanced and fair, communicating it by phone or e-mail to the original offender requesting damage control, and following up on the broadcast list to make certain that the issues were, in fact, cleaned up.

More internal wars have been started by e-mail than any other corporate weapon. What may appear to one person as short, crisp, and efficient is curt, rude, and dismissive to the recipient viewing it on a computer screen. Also what may have been intended as just a little sarcastic humor can unintentionally hit a sore spot. When the one-line message "You ought to be on Ritalin" appeared on the screen of an energetic manager, she was hurt. So she fired off her response, "WELL, YOU OUGHT TO BE ON PROZAC!!!!"

Consider too, that each e-mail sent requires work on the part of the person receiving it. It has to be retrieved and read with decisions made on what to do with the information.

Parties going through a divorce are finding that e-mail is often a good method of communicating with their estranged spouse. Rather than an angry, emotional exchange in person, e-mail affords an opportunity to write down an angry response and then sleep on it. A rewrite in the morning can take the emotion and hurt out of it. E-mail then becomes proactive in resolving issues, not reactive. Because it is a medium that lends itself to permanent data, it can be easily documented. Court dates, dollar amounts, and temporary custody arrangements are in black and white.

A Classic E-Mail Case Study

To: A long list of internal managers and executives, except the one person who could address the situation

From: One field sales person

Subject: Do we have a quality program in place at Rocky Top???????!!!!!

Dear Managers,

This information is going to blow you away. This is a description of what happened when one of our big customers received a shipment from one of our units. I was appalled by the total disregard for sending out a quality product. If we are going to put the Rocky Top brand on this unit's product, we damn well better do a better job of ensuring that we supply a quality product.

They received our product with the label upside down, a screw loose, and two bent items. They don't want shipment of any more junk. This is terrible. When will we get it right? Why are we selling this product? This customer has a long history of dissatisfaction with Rocky Top and I am not confident we can keep them as a customer. In a word, I'M JUST FED UP!!

This e-mail was broadcast to over 30 people, except the president of that divisional unit. When one of the recipients forwarded the e-mail to him, he read it, controlled his temper, got his facts from his engineers and quality control department, picked up the phone and called the sales person—as opposed to immediately blasting off a response.

The president was direct but calm. On the phone, the salesperson was much less confrontational and even rather embarrassed. After the phone call, the president did follow up with an e-mail and a plan for damage control.

To: The field sales person

From: The unit division president

Subject: We do have a quality program in place at Rocky Top

I wanted to respond to your e-mail regarding the quality issues you raised. I feel strongly that Rocky Top needs to maintain a positive relationship with our customers and the sales force. Sometimes we drop the ball. But we do have a track record of doing whatever it takes to solve the problem and make the customer satisfied.

We grew at a 40 percent rate last year and there were some quality problems. However, last month we were the highest rated in quality of all the business units so we are making progress.

I am concerned with some of the negative comments made in your last e-mail. Please understand that when negative accusations are widely distributed from our own sales force, it makes it very difficult to handle the damage control issues that sometimes occur from erroneous perceptions. Like other business units, we are competing for mind share. If the sales force ends up being turned off to our product line, we all lose. In these tough times of global competition, we can't afford to lose any opportunity for the wrong reasons. Bad news travels fast. Even via our competition. We need to be sure that what is widely circulated is accurate and solution driven.

On the phone, we addressed each of your quality issues. I have reviewed them in the attachments.

I would like to suggest that in the future, if there are issues that need to be resolved with Rocky Top products, please contact me directly. I will be responsive. But I want to avoid broadcasting e-mails that have little positive value and can, in fact, be divisive. Hopefully, after our phone call and the attachment, you will agree that the quality issues weren't as dismal as you originally thought.

Also I need your plan for damage control to clear up inaccuracies that occurred in your original e-mail. This will then need to be forwarded to everyone on the original list who received your first e-mail.

Please let me know if you would like to meet in person with your customer at our location. I would be happy to arrange a personal tour of our plant, including our quality control program.

Regards,

The president

Swift and competent handling of damaging, broadcast e-mails is part of maintaining professional presence. Don't allow erroneous information about you, your team, your product, or your company to float unrestricted in cyberspace.

Best Practices

Here is our list of Best Practices for e-mail etiquette that allow this truly incredible technology to work in our best interests:

1. Be extremely careful in using certain keys or functions:
   - The bold key, the underline key, and the all caps key are the equivalent of shouting at someone. The exception is their use in titling a document.
   - The exclamation point is often used to show anger and frustration.
   - The broadcast list function can either save time or clog up the server and burden all the recipients with yet one more e-mail to read.
   - The send key sends without any possibility of retrieval.

   Emoticons are typed symbols that attempt to add emotion or more dimension to e-mails. : --) when viewed sideways is a smiley face. Special groups use them too. \ / \ / \ / \ / and \/\/\/\/ are emoticons that owners of Labrador retrievers use to show slow and fast tail wags. Like a strong spice in cooking, a very small pinch is usually enough. They work better for personal e-mails than business ones.

2. Determine if e-mail is the best way to communicate a message. Sometimes picking up the phone and speaking with someone directly will result in a more expedient and satisfactory solution.

3. Make absolutely certain that your information is accurate. Because e-mail can be printed, archived, forwarded, and broadcasted, it becomes a permanent, unerasable document with your name attached to it. Contrary to what the delete key says, e-mail is never permanently deleted and can be retrieved.

4. If you are angry or emotional, don't send an e-mail. Cool off, sleep on it, and then reconsider your response. Once you have determined your response, put yourself in the receiver's place and determine how you would feel receiving it.

5. Reread each e-mail for spelling errors and correct grammar. E-mail is often treated like a "flow of consciousness." In this mode, the attitude can be that if a word is misspelled, so be it. However just as letters shouldn't go out with misspelled words, incomplete sentences, the wrong punctuation, or grammatical errors, e-mail should be afforded the same attention.

6. Keep it fairly short and friendly. Many people limit their e-mails to what can be viewed at one time on the screen. Others limit it to two pages. In any case, don't create an attachment if you can get the same information in the body of the e-mail, unless formatting is important. Then an attachment with bullets and tabs will look and print much better.

7. Be discriminating when attaching lengthy attachments. They take time to download, especially in remote locations, and time to read. Also, make certain that you attach the correct document.

8. Consider the volume of e-mail a recipient receives before inclusion in a broadcast list. Also consider if a "cc:" is really a "CYA."

9. Be extremely wary of sending anything that could be viewed as sexist, sexual, racist, or disparaging to others. A number of Fortune 500 companies have had to fire employees when it was documented that they e-mailed trade secrets, sent racist jokes, or engaged pornographic sites. The stakes are very high in terms of what employees can and can't send via company communications. Aside from losing important proprietary information, lawsuits addressing a "hostile workplace environment" can lead to million-dollar lawsuits.

> A CFO unintentionally attached the wrong salary information to a confidential e-mail. Instead of sending just one department's salary information to the manager of that department, he mistakenly attached "Salary2" instead of "Salary1" and forwarded the salaries of everyone in the entire company.

10. Be very careful about marking something "urgent." Use this warning only when it is required.

11. If you have not had any correspondence with someone, introduce yourself with your first e-mail by identifying your company, a mutual colleague, an area of interest, your background, or some important linking.

12. Always update or complete the subject heading on the e-mail. The subject heading should be indicative of the content of the e-mail. This courtesy will help individuals who receive numerous e-mails each day to prioritize those which need action first.

13. If you only e-mail someone periodically, use a greeting and a closing.

14. If you are in constant and consistent e-mail relationships with data going back and forth many times in one day, it is not necessary to use a greeting every time. However, it is polite to do a brief sign-off, like a simple "Thanks." In face-to-face communication, we have body language to communicate humanness. In voice mail, we have words.

15. If you set up telephone or in-person appointments using e-mail, be certain to follow up to confirm with a phone call. Systems and servers go down and nothing is totally foolproof—technology or one's memory.

16. Be sure to check your e-mail at least twice a day and more if you receive time-sensitive information. If you are not able to check your e-mail for a period of time be sure to leave an outgoing message indicating the date when you will be reading and responding to your messages.

17. Keep communication clear by marking your e-mail message with FYI or the action that you require. It is important to be thorough and explicit in your communication by directing the recipient on what to do with the information you have provided.

18. Company e-mail is just that. It belongs to the company. They are paying for it and providing the systems to send and retrieve it. Company e-mail isn't intended for privacy and doesn't provide it. In fact almost 30 percent of companies regularly monitor e-mail according to the American Management Association. If you want absolute privacy, register for your own account, paid for by you and accessed only on your home computer.

E-Mail Impact

The opportunity to access scores of experts on a specific topic is one of the dramatically beneficial ways that e-mail is being used. In progressive companies, managers are internally registering their competencies online and literally becoming online coaches and subject matter experts.

Dana Kuebler, assistant vice president for an insurance company, often gets e-mails with lists of questions like "How would you handle this project?" and "How do I go about setting up this type of system?" or "What's the best way to float bonds?"

When seeking information, the best format is questions that involve more objective feedback than subjective feedback. Questions and issues that require analysis, logic, and direct feedback work the best. When the resolution is more binary, more black and white, e-mail coaching is a terrific medium for determining the "Best Practices," the optimum method for procedures and handling situations. Dana indicates that she answers each as thoroughly as if she were in an interview. "I've found that this information often gets forwarded to other people in the organization. What I write and how I write it is a reflection of my professionalism. I give how tos, examples, resources, and reference tools in addition to my explanation. I've received feedback indicating that 'I know my stuff' just based on the way I answered the questions."

Much faster than the post office, more original than faxing, and formatted for brevity, productivity, and attachments, e-mail allows us to write more, respond faster, and actually create levels and volumes of business connection never before experienced. As long as we don't overuse it and remember when the human moments of face-to-face or phone-to-phone communications can work better, e-mail will continue to serve us well. It will broaden our professional base, extend our international reach, and allow us flexibility, autonomy, and influence in our work.

Forty-three percent of respondents to a recent *PC Magazine Online* poll indicated they get ten or fewer e-mail messages a day and seven percent said they get more than 75 messages daily. Thirty-two percent reported that they receive between 11 and 25, and 18 percent said they get between 26 and 75.
—*PC Magazine,* 1999

Step Four

Understand Business Etiquette

ten 10

Effective Meeting Management

Undertake not what you cannot perform; but be careful to keep your promise.

—*Manners, Culture and Dress, 1890*

Business historians tell us that Henry Ford insisted on being the only person who had a chair at his staff meetings. Everyone else stood. That eccentric technique did more than symbolize Ford's total control over his employees: It also kept meetings with him brief and to the point.

Every day we are blasted with committee meetings, board and staff meetings, online meetings, department and sales meetings, and team meetings—the list is endless. Meetings can become the black hole of modern business life. They can swallow time and zap energy. Or they can connect people and communicate information in ways that technology can't.

David Miller, the COO of a California-based high-technology firm, shared his efficient style: "When I first joined the firm, I told my department heads that I expected our twice weekly meetings to last no longer than thirty minutes tops. They all nodded and promptly

Standing up works in many areas of business. If you stand up when you're on the telephone, you will sound more alive, more vibrant, and will finish the conversation much quicker. Stand up in meetings. Take all the chairs out of the room. Believe me, nobody will be willing to listen to someone go on for hours when everyone is standing up.
—Greg Vetter, *Find It in 5 Seconds*

A Swiss executive moved to the United States. When his new boss asked how he was adjusting to the American business culture, he replied that the most difficult adjustment was how meetings were handled in the United States. In Switzerland, formal, written notification is given two weeks in advance and a detailed agenda is disseminated one week before. At the stated time of the meeting, everyone shows up early and the doors are locked one minute after the beginning of the meeting so latecomers are not allowed in. Pagers and cell phones are turned off. No one enters to interrupt the meeting or leaves the meeting early. It always ends on time.

In comparing this to how meetings are run in the United States the contrast is almost comical!

dismissed the idea. Department tradition had established that two-hour meetings were the norm.

"At my first early morning meeting, I took off my watch, in a kind of grand gesture, and placed it on the table. After twenty-five minutes had passed, I told my group that the meeting needed to end in five minutes. Five minutes later, I gathered my papers, smiled broadly and said the meeting was over, wished them a good afternoon and walked out.

"I left behind a slightly stunned and bewildered group of managers. As I left I said, 'Thirty minutes is plenty of time to do everything that's important. It just doesn't allow much time to waste. Let's be prepared and stay focused next time.'"

David sent a short e-mail the next morning to his entire staff restating his point of view. "I respect you and your time. Both are too valuable to spend in meandering discussions. Let's have an agenda and stay focused." His second session that week ended 27 minutes after it started, accomplished specific goals, and created a new fan club. No one meandered, no one showboated, and everyone was prepared.

One of our clients has a company-wide policy of holding three-minute meetings every morning to bring the team together, establish daily goals, and create esprit de corps. The writers of the television series "Hill Street Blues," started each police department episode with this same abbreviated meeting. Keeping meetings short and sweet establishes a tone of efficiency.

Get to the Point

Successful meetings are brief, focused, and productive. They happen by design, not by inadvertence. The objective of any meeting is action. Ego building and posturing never accomplish anything productive. Professionalism helps transform meetings from empty time-wasters into creative events.

Overly long meetings exhaust energies by extending stressful situations, lengthening detailed discussions, and meandering along without direction. They are also extremely costly. A gathering of eight middle- and upper-management people can cost a company literally thousands of dollars per hour unless they create clear, actionable deliverables.

Simian Behavior

Meetings also have other hidden costs. Gathered around a conference table, calm and otherwise rational people can tend to function as members of a primitive pack, much like the simian behavior seen in apes and monkeys. Some of these pack instincts are harmless or even amusing, like a young employee trying to act and talk exactly like the boss.

Other, more subtle behavior that mirrors the group can be useful. But in the absence of a leader who exhibits professionalism, balances the emotional needs of a group, and keeps rowdy team members in line, polarization and poor decisions are made. Often arising from threats to status or territory or an insistence on being "right" on an issue, such struggles generate friction and disruptive behavior and force the group into choosing sides.

Some instinctive imitation helps produce cooperation. Other instincts lead members of the pack to struggle and berate each other, sometimes savagely. As members of a corporate or organization team, we need to understand that the pack mentality is part of our professional context. When we focus its energies and blunt its ferocity,

Try this experiment at your next staff meeting. During a lull, make eye contact with someone across from you and casually pretend you are brushing a crumb from the side of your mouth. A few seconds later, do it again. You probably won't have to do it more than two or three times before the person sitting across the table subconsciously starts to imitate you. It may be because they think you are giving them a non-verbal clue to get the crumbs off their face. It may be because we tend to copy other people's behavior, sometimes on a purely unconscious level. Despite centuries of civilization, humans will instinctively imitate other humans.

we either keep control of the meeting if we are the leader, or maintain our status as an active participant.

For example, if one of the members makes an inappropriate comment such as, "Linda, you are so naïve and this idea of yours is really stupid," the leader of the meeting should immediately react: "Hey Peter, that remark was uncalled for. Let's keep this meeting on a professional level, not a personal one." The strong leader will not allow the remark to be endorsed or sanctioned by others. The leader should not even wait for others to nod in silent agreement to the inappropriate outburst.

As participants, we also have a responsibility to use our nonverbal responses carefully, accurately, and fairly. If the leader makes a scathing remark that is unjust or inaccurate to one of the participants, a strong, disapproving look back to the leader is appropriate. Also a remark like, "Excuse me, you have that information wrong," delivered calmly and with eye contact is apropos when defending yourself in front of others. A remark like, "I don't think that's accurate. Can we discuss it after the meeting?" will help make certain that you don't lose credibility.

> A good leader publicly apologizes for any deriding remarks.

When the reaction is more nonverbal, like scoffing or rolling of the eyes by other participants when a junior member makes a remark, it is still the responsibility of the meeting leader to address this either verbally or nonverbally. "Is there a problem, Peter, with John's remark?" If the leader doesn't address it or is too intimidated, then the other attendees should make it clear with their questioning looks that belittling attitudes are not appreciated and that they don't share that same, unjust opinion.

A good leader publicly apologizes for any deriding remarks. "Linda, I'm sorry that remark was made. It was totally uncalled for and we welcome your ideas."

Creating an environment of equality, where all ideas are viewed fairly no matter who contributes them, requires that the group's energies are focused in positive, productive ways. It is the responsibility of both the leader and each participant to see that the meeting is conducted in a professional manner.

The Powerful Participant

You may recall that the wizard Merlin won a prominent place in myth and legend by advising King Arthur to seat his knights at a round table. The world's first expert on group dynamics, Merlin theorized that a round table would blur inter-knight status distinctions. He was right, and the principle is still valid today.

Unfortunately, most modern conference rooms feature rectangular tables. Such clearly defined space triggers territorial instincts and exaggerates differences in rank. The head of the table is the "power perch." It is reserved for the most senior person present. The three other important positions are those to the right of the power perch, the seat to the left, and unless it is too far away, the seat opposite. However, it is not uncommon for the person who called the second meeting to sit at the head of table. Due respect should be given to the most senior person by inviting him or her to sit to the right of the power perch.

> The standing ovation started in ancient Rome when spectators rose to their feet to show appreciation.

If you are new to the organization and uncertain about your place at the table, hover around the coffee and doughnuts, examine the conference room's paintings, or admire the view. Better yet, take the opportunity to review your notes or to greet others standing in the room. Wait and watch to learn the seating protocol from more long-time attendees and then take your seat.

If you are seated when an important person enters the room, stand up to shake hands. For the past four thousand years standing up to acknowledge someone has been a show of respect. It still is today. And a woman should rise as readily to her feet as any man.

Here are some additional guidelines that will help you move to the head of the table while clearly showing your support for your boss.

- Sit as close to the leader as protocol permits. With physical proximity, you demonstrate an implied closeness in ideas and values.
- Follow the leader. Without looking like a mime, mirror and match the energy level of your superior. Also, if the leader uses

One of our trainers presented a seminar to about 25 people and encountered a very sticky problem. The decision maker who hired our firm talked to his zone manager the entire time. Our trainer finally stopped, looked directly at them, and with as much good humor as she could muster, asked, "Am I missing out on something? I hate it when that happens." They both replied, "Oh, no, we were just talking about how great this seminar is." It was a quick, probably inaccurate comeback, but more importantly, they refrained from their discussion for the rest of the presentation.

- formal conduct and speech, so should you. Keep in mind that this rule has its limits. The leader can sit on the corner of the table and appear confident and relaxed. If you do the same thing, you will appear disrespectful and insubordinate.

- Respect the leader. No daydreaming and no private, off-stage conversations with neighbors. If your boss is engaging in other conversation when you are making a presentation, you can either ignore it if it isn't lengthy, or simply stop talking and ask if they have a specific question.

- Discuss, but don't argue. Let others be right. When a leader has to constantly take time to break up arguments, time is wasted and reputations are tarnished.

- Sit with erect posture. Keep your feet under your side of the table and don't slump. Posture provides the context for everything said. Keep your arms on the table. Lean forward slightly with a bit of an angle to your head when you want to express interest. Moving physically closer, even slightly, increases the sense of involvement.

- Don't create subconscious, nonverbal barriers to communication. Be especially careful if you are in the habit of folding your arms across your chest.

- Demonstrate good energy and involvement. A high energy level is contagious. It is extremely appealing and a valued quality in a team player. A quiet energy level is also welcomed. Good listeners are usually able to process all the information that is thrown on the table and, with good analytical skills, come up with the right solutions.

Take a Stand

There is another aspect to being a powerful participant. Speak out! Take a stand! Sound off! Sometimes it is worth taking a calculated risk at a meeting because a confident leader likes to see certain strength of conviction. But taking risks requires that you do your homework. Don't spout off unless you know exactly what you are talking about and it doesn't directly contradict what the leader has just said.

Know, too, that introducing anything controversial will create tension. However, tension and a bit of rowdiness can produce innovative ideas as long as they are clearly summarized.

If a direct supervisor seems rude to you during a meeting, you have three options. You can ignore it and chalk it up to a bad day. You can confront the remark as soon as it is made. Or you can make certain that you meet immediately in private to discuss the issue. If you let it happen too many times without a comment, not only will your boss lose respect for you, you will lose respect for yourself.

Inconsiderate behavior perpetuates itself if ignored. One client explains, "I had a boss who felt a need to exert his rank from time to time. One way he did that was to arrive late for meetings. He felt that an important man like him was worthy of delaying the meeting for whatever reason (to get coffee, call his wife, or check voice mail). I realized that this was his occasional power trip. Sometimes I humored him and waited. But because I felt so angry to be kept waiting for

> Inconsiderate behavior perpetuates itself if ignored.

a meeting he called, I would often turn the tables. I'd just leave and he'd have to come find me for the meeting. I must admit that it was a subtle and destructive power struggle. It was resolved when I stopped the cycle by politely saying, 'I have some work to finish on the Jernigan account. Just let me know when you would like to start the meeting. I'll be in my office.' Or 'I'm ready when you are. I'll be in my office when you finish your calls.' This let him know, very clearly, that he was being rude to delay the meeting, and my work was important, too. Through this strategy, the relationship that was heading down a very destructive path was saved. This response created a win-win situation that valued each individual's time."

Meetings are a good place to showcase and self-promote. If you have developed a great idea for a new product or promotion, bounce it off a few trusted colleagues before bringing it before a larger group.

It is better to think through a plan and revise it or even get it totally shot down with some loyal friends than to misspeak in front of a larger, more public group.

A View from the Head of the Table

Let's set a hypothetical stage. You have just recently been promoted. Three other employees had hoped to win that job, but the decision was made to pick you. For two years you've been telling your outside business friends how much time the company wastes in meetings. Now it is time to call *your* staff together.

Incidentally, all three disappointed candidates will be waiting to see how you do. They have all shaken your hand and congratulated you. Now they are sitting back and secretly hoping that you will fall flat on your face. Instead, surprise them with your acumen.

1. E-mail a short memo prior to the meeting that targets each point you want to discuss. This allows each attendee to be prepared with suggestions and new ideas. It also shows that you, as the leader, have clearly thought through the agenda and are not wasting anyone's time.

2. Learn to pronounce everyone's name accurately. You will have more presence if you can call on every member using his or her first name. If a senior executive or outside person is attending the meeting, don't embarrass them by making them struggle with new, unfamiliar names. Use large tent cards placed in front of each attendee with their first name in large letters.

3. Understand what each person does so that you won't inadvertently step on toes. If you defer to someone else's advice, make sure that opinion is coming from a well-qualified source.

4. Be careful about personal comments, even those intended as "only kidding," until you know the group and its individual sensitivities very well. Extroverts often have to apologize and clean up a remark that shot out and landed too hard. Masculinity, femininity, age, weight, baldness, visual acuity, height,

and other physical or emotional attributes may be topics for banter among good friends. But with the possible exception of that peculiarly popular event known as the "roast," they are not appropriate for public comment in a new business environment.

A thoughtless comment is generally not meant as a personal attack. It was more of a "Do-Think-Do" response, meaning that being careless and impulsive eclipsed being careful and reflective.

5. Make certain that the meeting doesn't disintegrate into a lot of technical jargon or obscure references that only a few attendees understand. The leader has a responsibility to make sure that the communication is clear to everyone.

A Tale of Two Styles: Conflict and Consensus

First, Conflict

It is common, these days, for young senior staff members to have direct reports that are older than they are. These direct reports may have been passed over for promotion or simply declined them for a variety of reasons.

Douglas Girt was a confident thirty-one-year-old with an MBA from a prestigious university. He had been hired directly by the CEO of a large engineering firm. Doug was full of great ideas. He was also full of himself. As the new director of marketing, he felt he was just what the company needed to move forward with larger projects and greater revenues. From his perspective, the doddering fools who had formed the company 40 years ago needed to go.

Andrew had been with the company since he was 18 years old. He didn't have a college degree but had a

One of our clients made an off-hand comment that deeply offended another team member during a staff meeting. "Don't schedule a meeting during George's nap time," he said with a big smile. Although it was common knowledge that George took a short nap every day after lunch and despite the fact that the remark was made in good humor, George was mortified.

He received the comment as an assault on his virility and endurance. Despite an immediate and sincere apology by our client, that one careless public statement eroded their relationship until time, another apology, and a visible championing of one of George's good ideas at a staff meeting smoothed things over.

35-year perspective of the company's personnel, their products, and their client base. Andrew's tribal knowledge was vast. Doug felt competitive immediately. Rather than getting Andrew on his side, he demonstrated thinly veiled contempt at the first staff meeting.

Doug ignored the fact that Andrew had a long-term relationship with many employees. Their loyalty was with Andrew. Doug had the title and authority, but being new, had yet to earn the respect of his staff. With diplomacy and skillful management, he could have earned that respect and made an ally of Andrew. He could have deferred to Andrew in specific areas of his expertise during staff meetings and gained the respect of the group. He could have shown a little humility and said something like, "I have a great deal to learn about this company and I will need your help. In return, I will trust you to do your job and will be here for you when you need perspective. " Instead he chose confrontation at staff meetings.

By his visible lack of respect for the elder statesman, Doug inevitably started a chain reaction. Andrew and his supporters began to mutter among themselves at meetings. Without being openly defiant, their body language became negative when Doug spoke. They started quietly sabotaging every new idea outside the meeting.

In response, Doug got tough. He made his orders clear. In subsequent meetings, he physically moved around the table, telling Andrew and the others exactly what he expected of them—indeed, what he demanded of them. He had a visible revolt at every meeting, not in words, but in nonverbal behavior that included slouched posture, hands behind the head, and meaningful glances among the members. Several staff members stayed on their computers for the duration of the meeting.

Second, Consensus

Skilled leaders do not have to demand what they want from their groups. They demonstrate it. This principle is practiced by experienced meeting managers throughout the world.

Martin R., producer of a popular television show, is skilled at obtaining consensus. Using a great deal of grace and respect, he brought a group of writers and VIPs into agreement on a hotly controversial issue: whether or not to replace the co-star of a popular series.

In this process, Martin initially framed the situation and then spent most of the remainder of the meeting time listening. He made sure that everyone was heard—not just the most vocal ones. He put the spotlight on everyone. He occasionally reminded the group about budget constraints, production lead times, and other casting considerations. When the group started to digress, Martin brought them back to the topic at hand. Each member of the group spoke at least once; all expressed strong opinions. Their final decision, determined by consensus, was completely in accord with the producer's position.

"Congratulations, Marty," his head writer said to him the next day. "You finally got everyone's unanimous support for a co-star that needed to be fired. You are a born leader!"

"Thanks for the compliment, but the team really solved the problem. They are all talented people and they want the show to stay on top of the ratings," he said. "I just gave them some of the facts. They supplied the rest. My job was to keep the meeting focused, let everyone speak, not take sides, and sum up the conclusion accurately."

Marty left unsaid that he had also respected everyone's territory and status. With that foundation, he had only to focus their energies, preserve their sense of purpose, and summarize the prevailing viewpoint at the conclusion. By safeguarding each member's viewpoint, he was able to rely on commitment to team goals.

> The person in charge doesn't need to sit at the head of the table. You can sit like a participant—at the side of the table. The job of a leader is not to be the decision maker, but to get everyone speaking and contributing. Ask people who aren't talking what they think. It's hard to get introverts to pipe up. Have an outside facilitator lead the group if the issues are sensitive and critical. Meetings with more than 10 people usually don't accomplish a great deal.
> —Trish Zuccotti, Partner, Deloitte & Touche

How to Effectively Lead a Meeting

The concepts of handling a meeting professionally are sometimes subtle and often challenging. To be effective, they must be expressed and reiterated in concrete, tangible ways.

The following list is drawn from the experience of a number of highly successful meeting managers—people like Martin. Their ideas and suggestions have been proven in many business environments, with a variety of products and services and with widely diverse teams.

I tell people, "If you want to come to my meeting, tell me what value you are going to add. Show up prepared and make sure your presentation is in a format that can be read and understood by everyone." How many times have you been in a meeting and the presenter tells you to read the overhead and it is incomprehensible? I also insist that people are on time and stick to the time allotted for their part of the meeting. Meetings without agendas are canceled. A meeting without an agenda will not be efficient or effective for anyone.
—National Sales Manager for American Express

Eighteen Ground Rules for Meetings

1. Start on time; end on time. If the group gets onto an interesting or vital topic at the end of the meeting, table it for another time or ask if everyone can stay 15 more minutes to wrap the session up.
2. Provide a written agenda and stick to it. Even if the agenda lists only a few items, it will show you to be an organized, directed leader. Be careful. Allowing too much digression from the agenda detracts from your focus and your strength as a leader. Also be realistic. Most people won't do a lot of preparation before the meeting unless you request it individually and specifically.
3. Reserve the most comfortable, spacious conference room; however, if the table is too wide, there will not be a feeling of coming together and cohesiveness. It should have windows, well-padded chairs, and room for everyone to spread out. Make sure the room temperature and lighting are appropriate. The best speaker will lose an audience if participants feel that their physical comfort is being ignored. Make it easy to stay attentive.
4. Get there early to make certain that there is no debris left from the previous occupants. Dry eraser boards should be clean. Extraneous flip charts should be removed. Used coffee cups and refreshment remnants should be gone. Make sure that community clean-up is part of how you end your meetings.

5. Serve refreshments that are tasty, fresh, and fairly easy to eat. Everyone appreciates hospitality. Have them available on the conference table on a self-serve basis. However, if you have scheduled a fairly long meeting, have the food and beverages close by so that participants can stand up, stretch a bit, and easily access the food.

6. Don't recap information for latecomers. They can learn everything they need from someone else later. Your summary represents tacit approval of their tardiness, is boring to those who already heard the information, and doesn't deliver the appropriate consequence for showing up late.

7. Stand up and go to a flip chart or marker board when you want to make an especially important point or need visual explanation. Standing up makes you at least twice as tall as anyone else in the room. Moving the focus from you to the flip chart changes the energy in the room. It also emphasizes the commitment you have to the statement you are making.

8. Don't rush. You want to keep the meeting upbeat and moving swiftly, but if you speak too quickly you may appear insecure and frightened. The "pregnant pause" is good drama and a highly effective attention-getter. Don't interrupt. Allow everyone to be heard.

9. Observe the audience. Watch body language. Is someone looking confused after you have made a point? Stop and ask questions. Find the source of their puzzlement and resolve it. Are they bored? Revive their active participation by asking specific questions or taking a break.

10. Control your hands. Don't click pens, fold and unfold paper, twist your hair, or fiddle with your clothing. Keep your wrists firm when gesturing. Always keep your hands on the table and visible.

11. Keep facial expressions positive and attentive. Others are likely to imitate both your expressions and your attitudes. While humor works, jokes don't.

12. Make strong, connected eye contact with each person at the meeting. Don't move on until you know the color of their eyes. Don't just sweep over the group and then bury your nose in your notes. And don't ignore people at the end of the table. If the room is in a "U" set-up, take advantage of it. Don't stand at the front of the room. Enter the U when you speak or present to enhance connectedness with the participants. If the table is too wide, change rooms. There will never be a cohesion in that environment.

13. Turn off cell phones and pagers and don't accept telephone calls during a meeting. Don't allow people to walk in and out of your meeting, or to pop in, even for "just a second." If you do, the meeting loses its momentum, the attendees lose their concentration, and the person in charge loses presence.

14. If you have to leave a meeting early, indicate the reason and be certain the transition is smooth. Leave at a break and don't linger to see how the person taking over is doing with the group. Abrupt leave-taking without an explanation will significantly diminish all the previous progress.

15. Be careful about overdoing clichéd sports-oriented terms to energize a group. Many women and some men find it tiresome and not at all inspiring. Too many coaching analogies like "Let's score a touchdown on that one, guys," or "We need to run pass interference" can be irritating. However, using real examples and stories, but choosing a variety of venues, is a powerful way to illustrate your points and gain consensus.

16. For meetings longer than one hour, allow sufficient bathroom, refreshment, and stretch breaks.

17. It is everyone's responsibility to stay on task. If someone gets off the topic, someone else—the leader or another participant—has to have the initiative to get the meeting back on track.

18. Always end with action steps. Otherwise, the meeting will have been a waste of time.

One manager who heads a public relations firm plays high powered dance music or show tunes and lets his people get re-energized at break. He doesn't use it all the time, but for long brainstorming or strategic sessions, it works great.

Break It Up

There is one other valuable technique for managing a meeting with presence, developed from an observation of jury behavior. Throughout the course of a trial, the 12 jurors generally form into several small cliques. Forbidden to discuss the trial, friendships still form with other jurors who may share the same values, background, work experience, and ideas. When moved into the jury room for deliberations, alliances are forged that started forming in the lunchroom.

> One manager who heads a public relations firm plays high powered dance music or show tunes and lets his people get re-energized at break.

In one reported case, the jury foreman was a capable and wise woman. After three hours of futile haggling, she called for a break. When the jury returned, she had written everyone's name on a separate place card and put the cards in front of different seats to scramble up the seating arrangement. By breaking up their comfortable seating, she broke up their physical connection with the clique.

One hour later, they had settled the case. But the deliverable was more than the jury verdict; the corporate world, too, learned a valuable lesson. Breaking up comfortable, established seating arrangements often breaks up obstructive alliances.

To maximize the benefit of your meetings, consider changing the location—maybe to an off-site location; the seating arrangements—maybe to a different table configuration, the leadership of the meeting—maybe rotating the leadership to other team members.

Valuable Opportunity

Meetings are a central part of communication and cooperation with any organization. They create the human, face-to-face moments that don't happen with e-mail, voice mail, and telephone conferences. Recognize that they present valuable opportunities to develop skills and build a reputation, as well as to stay on top of essential company information. Because they generally aren't permanently documented, like e-mail is, there is a freer exchange of information.

Whether as a strong leader or a powerful participant, savvy meeting skills will win recognition and respect for your strengths and your contributions.

eleven

11

Dangling Conversations: Gossip, Grapevine, and Jokes

Those who scatter brilliant jibes without caring whom they wound, are as unwise as they are unkind. Those sharp little sarcasms that bear a sting in their words, rankle long, sometimes forever, in the mind, and fester often into a fatal hatred never to be abated.

—*Manners, Culture and Dress, 1890*

A colleague just offered you a week at her condo on the beach in gratitude for handling her clients while she was away for a month. Or, the customer who has been your biggest source of revenue for the past year just declared bankruptcy. What's the first thing you want to do in either case? Tell someone, of course.

Celebrating, or commiserating, with office staff or colleagues helps us gain perspective on both triumphs and disasters. Talking things over with others helps to humanize the work and the workplace. One of the biggest reasons that virtual offices fail is simply because there is no one to talk to face to face. Not being able to walk into another cubicle to share exciting news, or sit down with a colleague and a cup of coffee and get a pep talk when things are going badly, is a distinct disadvantage.

143

On the other hand, companies point to idle chatter and water cooler gossip as one of the worst offenders that contribute to unproductive, wasted time. Vicious gossip has often been the cause of ruined careers, and whole companies have been adversely affected because of unfounded industry rumors. Procter & Gamble was impacted by several totally unfounded but widely circulated national rumors. In fact, it took Procter & Gamble ten years to finally win a judgment based on a "satanic" rumor that was started by just one couple in Topeka, Kansas.

The couple started a fax campaign to a number of their multilevel customers claiming the logo used by P & G represented a satanic image. Actually it was a design that Procter & Gamble had created over a century ago and was not at all connected with anything evil. Yet the rumor mill generated thousands of phone calls to Procter & Gamble by consumers who were concerned that corporate profits were going to the devil.

Handling Vicious Gossip

When an employee begins to lose credibility within the ranks because of unfounded gossip or rumor, or a broadcasted e-mail with inaccurate information, maintaining professional presence becomes critical. If you find yourself in that uncomfortable position, don't act too hastily. Don't curtail your activities or new projects because of criticism or gossip. Stay calm, think it through, and devise a strategy to get things back on track.

If possible, determine the person or persons who are the source of the unfounded information. Calmly confront the source of a rumor to counteract and control the damage. Because the tendency is to walk away from a conflict, it is often very disarming to be directly confronted by someone who has been wronged. Often the "rumor source" immediately apologizes and stops the flow of flawed information. Even if they react defensively and don't acknowledge it, chances are they will certainly back off. Although gossip cannot be entirely eliminated, we can learn to control it.

The president of a bank made the front page of the business section the same day he was to attend one of our seminars. In the write-up, the reporter indicated that he was rumored to be fired. The president called his PR department and asked where they had gotten this information. The assistant pulled up the file and revealed the source as one of the board members. Then our client, in his most calm and pleasant manner, called the board member and said, "The information in today's business section about my imminent demise from the bank has been traced to you. I wonder if you can tell me if it's true?"

The board member began to stammer, and then confessed to "misspeaking concerning the status of the bank president." He said he would call the newspaper with a corrected report that indicated the rumor wasn't true.

The Grapevine's Accuracy

When an organization is under stress, rumors abound and tempers run short. When unpopular decisions are made, like product lines being eliminated or mergers being considered, rumors come with the territory. In such an atmosphere, clear communication with people above and below you is especially important. With emotions having the capacity to taint the truth, it's essential to keep the facts straight.

> Most active boards of directors, including major investors, will have "ears" in a company.

There is good news and bad news about the office grapevine. The bad news is that it is impossible to dismantle, discourage, or get rid of it. The good news is that this informal communications network is usually over 80 percent accurate.

So don't tune out; it's better to tune in. Listening to the grapevine can help uncover poor attitudes, sabotaging managers, the real customer service complaints, and a host of other problems.

Most active boards of directors, including major investors, will have "ears" in a company. They want to know what is really going on, not just what the officers report. How else can they learn about a personality who is causing conflict in the operation? That kind of thing is seldom written in a memo.

One company that we work with has a board of directors who are also investors in the firm. They occasionally attend staff meetings and regularly take mid-level managers out to lunch, just to have regular chat sessions. Through grapevine information, they learn valuable data, which on a number of occasions was turned into sound decision making. When the directors learned from the mid-level staff that the company didn't need the complex technology "solution" that was part of a two-year installation, and in fact, shipping would be a fiasco during the installation time, the project was stopped for re-evaluation.

Other issues in the office can only be revealed through tuning into the grapevine. The employee's manual can't list the people who are best avoided. Be smart and tune in. The grapevine also can help you to understand where your company's true priorities lie. Often what is claimed to be company policy and what actually happens are two different things.

The "Mother Mary" Syndrome

Most businesspeople spend a third of their lives with their office family. They share confidences, victories, and insecurities. When you're new on the job, however, you need to be wary of the established employee who immediately latches on to you and tries to be the source of all information about everyone in the office. There may be a hidden agenda that will cause problems later.

In one Midwest manufacturing company there was a certain office manager who tried to manipulate all new hires. Everyone called her "Mother Mary" because of the way she attached herself to any new employee in a pseudo-nurturing manner.

She cornered newcomers in the hallway or at the water cooler, established a premature level of confidence by sharing office gossip and her evaluations of other employees. Unfortunately, she so prejudiced the new personnel in the office that they invariably started off on the wrong foot. She would establish an "us" against "them" environment.

Part of the problem was that none of her coworkers respected her or wanted much to do with her. But she wanted to be part of the office family, so she turned to the unsuspecting new employee who understandably wanted to make friends and become established. One interesting development was that the other employees began to watch new hires and judge their ability to size up a bad situation by how quickly they unhooked themselves from "Mother Mary."

Whether you are a new employee or not, if you find yourself the recipient of too much gossip about others, remaining noncommittal and a bit detached is the best option. You can diffuse the gossiper's effect with statements such as, "I really don't know Liz, so I'd like to form my own opinion about her." Or, "I've only met him briefly. He seems very capable."

> When employees want to commiserate with you about their difficult boss, their untalented administrative staff, or their minuscule merit raise, play the role of a concerned cousin, not an overly sympathetic parent.

Having power and presence means getting your own information from various sources before forming an opinion. Getting too cozy with someone you don't know and making judgments based on hearsay can be deadly to getting along with your office family as a whole.

When employees want to commiserate with you about their difficult boss, their untalented administrative staff, or their minuscule merit raise, play the role of a concerned cousin, not an overly sympathetic parent. Listen with concern, be part of the office family, but don't entangle yourself by offering too much advice.

When Too Much Is Revealed

Keeping personal secrets is difficult. Keeping professional secrets is even more difficult. However, since knowledge is power, it is a mistake to get loose-lipped and mention something of great sensitivity to an insensitive colleague that can then never be retracted. It is equally uncomfortable to know that someone has the "goods" on you.

Once private information has been passed on, it is no longer a secret. Research has determined that less than one percent of the population can keep a secret. Don't risk being the central topic of office gossip by sharing any information that could backfire.

If you have mistakenly shared too much personal information with the wrong individuals, or let something slip by accident, do damage control. Sit down with them, request confidentiality concerning what you disclosed, but don't show obvious signs of panic. Most businesspeople will show consideration and not repeat your secrets. The other, smaller percentage will repeat it anyway. All you can do when the wrong people know your secrets is to forgive yourself and vow to be more careful in the future.

If you need to confess or vent, seek out someone who is not connected professionally to you or your business and will remain loyal. Passing along information that could harm you now or years down the road is the calculated risk of letting down your hair too much. Nearly all of us do it. We need the intimacy of sharing concerns. We just need to be careful whom we choose and what we share.

Personal Issues to Avoid with All Clients and Most Colleagues

- Details of a pending divorce
- Bankruptcies
- Illicit affairs
- Confidential information known about bosses or coworkers
- Salary levels

Professional Issues to Avoid with All Clients, Although This Information May Be Carefully Shared with Appropriate Company Colleagues

- Client confidences
- Customer complaints
- Closely held company information, like the actual cost of goods for a best-selling product
- Sales figures that are not public knowledge

- New products that have not yet been introduced. Many computer companies have regretted sharing this type of information with customers. If a product on the drawing board is smaller, better, and cheaper, then why would a customer buy the existing product?

A client of ours told us that when a competitor confided to him that his company was having trouble with a new product, he was able to land a big order. He was amazed at how loose-lipped his competitor had been with highly confidential information.

During the sales call with the buyer they both called on, our client simply dropped a few hints about his competition's problems. The buyer decided not to hold back $250,000 of his budget waiting for a product that might be loaded with problems. Our client got the buyer to redirect the budget to his company.

Let the Grapevine Do the Talking

If you get invited to the boss's house and others in the office weren't, don't mention your good fortune. This is not the same as self-promotion. Similarly, if you received an invitation to attend a holiday party at a client's home and others involved with the client didn't, avoid the urge to brag about it. If you begin to play golf, tennis, or socialize on a personal level with the boss, or the boss's boss, the word will get around, and the grapevine will be a much more powerful acknowledgment of your success.

Know When to Hold 'Em, Know When to Fold 'Em

One of the rules of corporate conversation is not to communicate everything that comes to your mind. If someone has been mysteriously let go, don't fan the flames with, "I am pretty sure that she was embezzling from the company. She always looked too well dressed for her salary."

> In business, we will never go wrong if we are generous with praise and stingy in stating our own biases.

These kinds of remarks are not only pure speculation, they are also professionally naïve. If we can't clearly prove any public statement we make, we are contributing to gossip and discord. In business, we will never go wrong if we are generous with praise and stingy in stating our own biases. Sometimes we need to hold our cards close to the vest and keep personal opinions to ourselves.

Conversations in the Office: Dos and Don'ts

Knowing what to say, when to say it, and to whom is an art. Having the ability to enjoy a lively discussion with the mailroom clerk and then switch gears for a black-tie event with your boss requires skill in the technique of good conversation.

The basis of good conversation is discovering what makes the other person feel engaged and accomplished. Add an authentic, animated expression, don't interrupt, and make eye contact, and the speaker will see all the signs of a great listener. Your nonverbal communication will say that you are listening to someone who is smart, clever, and informed.

The weather is one topic that is presumed safe and therefore healthy for business. But even the safest of topics can be disastrous.

Meet Anthony Zone. He is a damage appraiser for an insurance company and usually works in the field. When he returns to the office on sunny spring days the secretaries make envious remarks about what a cushy job he has driving around in the sunshine while they're tied to their desks. He gets upset when they don't understand that his job entails fighting traffic, avoiding guard dogs in wrecking yards, and crawling around under cars—rain or shine. For Anthony and his coworkers, the weather is not a safe topic.

If you live in St. Petersburg or San Diego, don't compare the cold, the wind, and the snow of Chicago to your hometown when you call on a client in the Windy City. An attendee at one of my seminars told me that he really put his foot in his mouth when he joked about Michigan's crummy, cold weather and Atlanta's 250 days of sunshine during a training session he did for a Detroit automobile company. His Detroit colleagues were not amused. In fact, he spent the rest of his time there trying to make up for initially rubbing everyone in the class the wrong way.

Sports are usually an interesting topic of conversation. Although some men and women don't avidly follow sports, smart businesspeople will read at least the front page of the sports section to know which teams are playing. Knowing just a few highlights, they will be able to either initiate or enter the conversation should it turn to athletics. Keeping up with a customer or colleague's sports interest serves as a form of courtesy.

Cars can be an enticing topic. Automobiles are general enough, fairly noncontroversial, and most people own one. But don't bring up cars just to talk about your new Jaguar.

Families and children are great as a topic, but only if clients or coworkers have children, too, or show a keen interest. Cute stories about one's children create boredom if your conversational partner lives in a singles' complex downtown and plays racquetball for three hours every evening.

You can certainly ask coworkers or clients about their plans for the weekend. This will generally provide fertile ground for more conversation. At a networking meeting, one of our clients was talking to the branch manager, who looked as though he might do a lot of hunting and fishing. When asked what he was planning to do over the weekend, he said he was going to a flamenco dancer's convention in Canada. They had a great time discussing his surprising avocation.

> Families and children are great as a topic, but only if clients or coworkers have children, too, or show a keen interest.

Weekend activities can give you a window into an individual's personal life and create lively conversation without having to get too nosy. One of our clients is an avid collector of curiosities on the weekends. He owns a bed that Al Capone slept in. He describes it as a rather small little number with a great deal of lapis and gold gilding. He also has a nearly complete set of the original Hardy Boys books. This opens doors for him into most informal conversations.

Staying Informed

Current events are usually good topics. But if you're the one introducing them, stay neutral. Don't be too opinionated on any subject until you are certain your opinion will not antagonize clients or colleagues.

Reading your daily newspaper, *USA Today* or the *Wall Street Journal*, or popping up the news on the Internet, gives an important update on world events. Watch news programming like Headline News, CNN, or any of the morning shows, especially in their first hour of broadcasting, will make certain that you are not in the dark about vital, news-breaking issues.

It is critical that you stay informed about mergers, acquisitions, natural disasters, newly passed laws that affect businesses, major layoffs, major hiring and firings, recent IPOs, and current news about your customers. Businesspeople are deemed professional when they know what is happening in the world, are current on news events, and are knowledgeable on general business issues.

When the Justice Department started its investigation of Microsoft, the coverage was so thorough and the impact on everyone was so enormous, that it astounded the entire table when a trainer at a major computer company stopped the conversation with a, "Now, what's happened at Microsoft?" Nearly everyone outside the computer industry knew many of the details of the anti-trust suit. Within the industry, nearly all computer company employees were following it with avid interest.

> Even with busy lives, most people will videotape a favorite show to stay current.

New television programs spark lively discussions. Even with busy lives, most people will videotape a favorite show to stay current. From prime time TV to PBS to what's on HBO this week, television shows offer a medium that invites comments and lively conversation.

The theater, symphony, ballet, and opera are rich topics, but only if your partner in conversation is an avid fan. Even if you know nothing about these things, being able to ask a few right questions and listening intently is all that is required.

"Where did you go to school?" is not an inquiry about where you spent the first 12 years of your education. It is only an appropriate question if you are certain the person went to college, and if you haven't prejudiced yourself beforehand about any school. Some professionals will wear a college ring in business simply as a way to begin a conversation and thus cultivate a business relationship.

Current best-selling business books are always a good bet. So are movies. But if you loved a movie, like *Apocalypse Now,* and your client hated it, don't lobby for your point of view unless it is done in exceedingly good humor. Restaurants, vacations, and leisure activities are also easy to discuss.

Dangerous Conversations

When controversial topics like abortion, gun control, capital punishment, animal rights, or international trade policies are introduced, it's best to stay neutral if you are with customers. Even if you have strong opinions, you can win the battle and lose the war should you belong to the opposite camp. If you find out with certainty that you are in the same camp with your customer, then you can carefully offer your viewpoint.

Avoid discussions of personal medical issues. No one really cares whether you have shin splints or a sinus infection. Sharing the details of gall bladder surgery or a push-by-push account of a difficult labor is never good office or cocktail conversation.

Sexual conversation is usually a mistake. Discussing your vasectomy with a group of women could easily be misinterpreted. One of our clients attended a dinner with six other businesspeople when one of the guests pulled out a sex quiz that had appeared in that month's issue of *Cosmopolitan* magazine. She went around the table polling everyone about intimate issues that embarrassed her guests. She thought it would lighten up the conversation because the quiz was tongue in cheek, but her ill-conceived attempts to engage the group alienated everyone.

> Avoid discussions of personal medical issues.

Certainly both religion and politics are loaded and emotional topics. If you unexpectedly find yourself at odds with a client over any sensitive issues, quickly suggest "agreeing to disagree," and move the conversation onto safer ground. Ending with, "I certainly respect your position on that," or "A lot of people have that opinion," or "I can see your point" helps maintain a good relationship.

Certain discussions about the cost of things can be arrogant and inconsiderate. A conversation between a new accountant and a well-established restaurant owner demonstrates this. She was fretting over the maintenance cost of her Rolls Royce. The young accountant limply interjected that the tune-up on his Toyota was $198 and that seemed like a lot of money.

> Never discuss your income with anyone, except the IRS or your partner.

Talking about your housekeeper, nanny, gardener, personal trainer, or your investment banker to someone who has no need of, desire for, or ability to pay for these particular services is snobbish and rude. What is the point of clearly pointing out different socioeconomic levels except to embarrass? Rarely is anyone of quality ever impressed. It just widens the distance between people instead of getting them on the same page.

Never discuss your income with anyone, except the IRS or your partner. Net worth is no yardstick of real worth, despite what the arbitrageurs try to tell the world. Either you are making more money or less money than the person you are talking to is making. Where do you go from there except to start to compare "toys"?

Name-Dropping

In many corporate and societal circles, name-dropping is common and pervasive. It creates a potential connection and shows the kind of company that one keeps. However, dropping names as an attempt to impress others looks either desperate or insecure.

As business becomes more complex and diversified, we need as many methods as possible to connect with others. While the Internet allows for significantly expanded e-mail communication, businesspeople still need to leverage their contacts. Appropriate name-dropping allows a kind of connecting between people who usually don't know each other at all. It can create an entrance into a relationship that would otherwise not happen. It also provides an affiliation and can, at the very least, keep a conversation going.

The only safe way to drop names is authentically. At Bonne Bell Cosmetics, people would say they regularly ran 10K races with the company president, "Jesse" Bell. People in the company knew they hadn't even shared a cup of Gatorade. The reason was simple: No one ever called him "Jesse." He was always called Jess.

When she was active in the running of the company, no one who knew Estée Lauder ever referred to her as Estée. She was always referred to as Mrs. Lauder. William Buckley Jr.'s very social wife is known as Mrs. Buckles or Patsy in New York circles. But if someone says they know Patty Buckley, it is a sure giveaway that they never met her.

It is more powerful to have your associations with others revealed discreetly through a longer relationship than sheer name-dropping would permit. But business moves too quickly and relationships must be forged when the moment presents itself. So if you know a prominent businessperson, or have even attended the seminar of a well-known speaker and engaged in a five-minute conversation after the presentation, use the experience to your professional advantage.

> It is more powerful to have your associations with others revealed discreetly through a longer relationship than sheer name-dropping would permit.

The Pitfalls, Limitations, and Realities of Office Romance

At first sight it would appear as if both love and marriage were beyond the rules of etiquette; but it is not so. In society we must conform to the usages of society, even in the tender emotions of the heart.

—Manners, Culture and Dress, 1890

Amanda and her boss, Bill, worked for a management company. After two years of working together, Amanda invited Bill to her home for dinner. That began a very intense relationship that could have potentially destroyed their careers. But once they knew a strong relationship was inevitable, they mapped out a strategy to keep both romance and careers intact.

Bill told his boss exactly what was happening and secured his promise to keep it confidential. Bill and Amanda agreed that no e-mails, cards, fax transmittals, or intimate phone conversations would take place in the office. They also agreed not to pull any stunts like going into the stockroom together, locking the door, and not emerging for 45 minutes. Bill resolved to be a little more visibly demanding on Amanda at work, just to be certain that no one accused him of favoritism.

One year later they announced their impending marriage to the flabbergasted office staff. No one had suspected that Bill and Amanda even liked each other. Bill definitely did not play favorites because he frequently gave Amanda the least desirable assignments. Amanda seemed personally indifferent to Bill, although she was a loyal team member.

Love in the Office

Handling chemistry at the office is part of maintaining professionalism. An office romance is bound to happen at one time or another in every businessperson's career. Either it will happen to you or to someone in your company whom you know well. The issue is not that it happens but how well it is handled.

If we define ourselves by our work, as many do, then seeing the traits and characteristics in others that we value or strive for in ourselves can be exciting. Self-confidence, intelligent decision making, creativity, poise, charisma, charm, and adept people skills are alluring traits that can be a potent magnet in the workplace.

> Self-confidence, intelligent decision making, creativity, poise, charisma, charm, and adept people skills are alluring traits that can be a potent magnet in the workplace.

There is also a power aspect. Dating a superior or a superstar at the office has an allure. It is similar to a freshman dating a senior in high school. Sometimes it is almost a mentoring relationship, wherein the junior person learns firsthand from an executive. The junior person is exposed to positioned people, exclusive locations, and high-powered situations where he or she normally would not have access.

Often, the excitement of being on a team and making things happen can form a powerful bond. When a large sale happens, the feeling of euphoria can stir up romantic feelings that might previously have been held in check. Professional admiration can turn into something more.

It's Not a Meat Market, But It Is a Meet Market

With the number of hours that most professionals devote to their careers, it is natural that we look for dates and potential spouses at work. Who has the time, energy, or ego to waste at the bar scene?

> With the number of hours that most professionals devote to their careers, it is natural that we look for dates and potential spouses at work. Who has the time, energy, or ego to waste at the bar scene?

The reality is that romance at the office is as common as laptops. More romances start in the office than in any other environment. Often people will interview at a particular company solely because it has the reputation for employing a high caliber of individual. Why not take advantage of a company's professional screening process to work alongside the best and the brightest? For someone new to a city, this may be the only safe place to find a date.

So the environment is ripe. There is not the awkwardness of a blind date. We get to know our coworkers on a multidimensional basis and we usually see them at their best. The office is a place where productivity counts, and professional goals are often the same.

How Companies View Office Romance

Generally the smaller the company, the more office romances are tolerated. The environment is more casual, and in general there are significantly fewer rules and procedures.

But the larger a company and the more established it is, the more it covertly or very overtly discourages romance between employees. When a company does acknowledge the presence of romance, it often does a poor job of handling it. Employees may be belittled, transferred against their will to other departments, or snidely made the butt of office gossip. In the worst-case scenario, especially when one partner is more expendable, a firing occurs.

If a company has a clear "no fraternizing" policy, both employees risk immediate dismissal with few questions asked. One large firm where we consult has a clearly stated "no fraternizing" policy. When there are any known infractions, the respective bosses ask both parties into their office and give them one warning. Then the parties involved are told to go home for three days to think about it, and if they agree with the company's decision, they still have a job. But if the relationship continues, they are swiftly given the sack. The only way to save their careers is if one employee volunteers to leave the company. The policy is clearly made known at the time of hiring and is expected to be unconditionally followed.

Because of the size, position, and confidentiality of the information that this company handles, this policy has merit according to the CEO. "We could be sued if any of our stockholders knew that a love affair was going on between our employee and one of our vendors," states one of the company officers.

> The office romances that work are two people who leave the romance out of working hours.

Most companies have found that this is a difficult policy to enforce fairly. They have also found that they have lost some of their best employees because of it. In one department there was a significant "brain drain" because two experienced managers became involved with two salespeople, and the exit of four competent, well-trained, and romantically involved people left a gaping hole.

Also, if employees are forced to go elsewhere, they generally wind up at the competition, which is often a worse situation than having two involved employees together in the same office.

Rather than make romance a part of the rules and regulations, often companies tend to quietly discourage it. But when it does happen, they expect a certain level of professionalism to reign.

The office romances that work are two people who leave the romance out of working hours. As a litmus test, an outsider shouldn't see any indication that these two people are a couple. This is accomplished with few lunches together, no lounging around each other's cubicle, and little planning of social events during work hours except for an occasional phone call.

Birds and Bees of a Very Different Feather and Stinger

There is a big difference, professionally, between an employee dating a married person and two single people having a mutually agreed upon relationship. Simply stated, it is nearly impossible to recover completely from a married affair that becomes public. Once the word gets out, it is a much more tantalizing bit of news than the two single "new hires" heating it up at the company picnic.

Invariably, one of the employee's spouses will call the office, and unwitting office associates will spill the beans, or they will be in the awkward position of having to cover for their coworkers. More than one wronged spouse has angrily entered an office threatening harm and demanding a divorce. In fact, many offices are taking security precautions to prevent this type of domestic violence.

In one case a husband had found out that his wife was in the Virgin Islands the previous week with her male coworker although she had told her husband that she had a sales meeting in Toledo. She called home every day to allay suspicion, but then her husband stopped by the office to pick up her paycheck. When her assistant showed off a souvenir brought back from the Islands, the facts became clear, and the marriage ended.

> When an indiscretion is revealed, reputations are tarnished and professional stature can be permanently damaged.

Our culture respects loyalty and devotion. We highly regard people who can make a commitment to their spouse and to their job. Because of our value system, there is always a suspicion in everyone's mind when a married affair is revealed. If this employee can be disloyal to someone they promised to be committed to, they could be equally shallow and unfaithful to the company. When an indiscretion is revealed, reputations are tarnished and professional stature can be permanently damaged.

On the other hand, relationships between single people at most offices are generally acceptable if they are handled with discretion. If the romance ends, both parties can completely recover from a consenting relationship that went sour, if both parties maintain a civilized parting.

Keeping Your Cool When You're Not

All relationships require some ground rules. Office relationships require even more because of the added dimension of bosses, coworkers, customers, and income.

- At the onset of a relationship with a coworker, don't confide in anyone who could blackmail you, unfairly discredit your work, or spread rumors. Don't make any announcements or even discuss your relationship with coworkers until you are clear on the level of mutual commitment. Wait until you are both well past the euphoria of the first date.

- Once your romance is common knowledge, be comfortable with it. Try to maintain the same attitude and demeanor as before. The more natural you are around your significant other, the more quickly others will accept the relationship.

- If you decide not to disclose your romance to anyone, don't try to cover up the affair by casting aspersions on the character of your lover. Remarks like, "He's always saying stupid things at the staff meeting," or, "She is such a nag about office procedure" will backfire.

- Don't send e-mails. Unless they are from a personal account, e-mails are the property of the company and are permanently archived. They are rarely confidential and can be easily circulated around the office. One involved employee at a manufacturing company had her torrid message intercepted and the prankster broadcasted it to the entire company.

- Don't think you can make goo-goo eyes at your lover at the staff meeting and still maintain a professional reputation. Meaningful body language exchanges are as potent as words.

- Learn to be an actress or an actor to maintain a facade. You will be in many situations where you will have to convey feelings that don't exist and hide ones that do.

- Don't do anything that will generate jealousy from your loved one or from your staff. Flirting with a vendor in front of your significant other is an appalling mistake. Bragging about the hours you spent in the sun on a sailboat in Barbados with your romantic associate, will not endear you to the administrative staff.

- Love has the tendency to make us daydream and waste time. Create an environment that will keep you focused. Consider normal working hours off base for romantic exchange between two people in the same office. If nothing is communicated by memo, letters, flowers, or interlude, then there will be minimal impact on your work and on others.

All You Need Is Love . . . and a Boss Who Understands

In some cases it is wise and in other cases it is dangerous to disclose your romance to your boss. A large part has to do with your performance on the job, your boss's temperament, and the prior precedent that has been set for interoffice relationships.

Here are some of the pros and cons of revealing your affair to your boss:

Pros

- You appear straightforward, honest, and professional.
- It may save your job down the line if the romance sours.
- If a coworker brings it to the attention of your boss later, the issue will have already been discussed by the parties involved and the news won't take your boss by surprise.
- You have the chance to demonstrate how adept you are at handling difficult situations by making the boss aware of the romance, then handling it with great discretion.

Cons

- Your work may be more scrutinized and your boss may be more suspicious of requests for personal time off or an extended business trip.

- A longer lunch hour, late arrival in the morning, or frequent exits at 4:00 P.M. may cause misgivings, even if everyone else in the office does it.
- You may get transferred or moved to another position because your boss feels that your romance will put unnecessary stress on the rest of the staff.
- You may be fired.

Once an Affair Is Over

The most difficult part of an office affair is the aftermath. It is hard enough getting over a love affair without having to face that person in the office every day or even every week at the staff meeting. Probably the most important reason coworkers decide not to pursue a relationship is because of the ramifications of a breakup and not because they don't see the potential for a good romance.

Here are four principles to maintain until the emotional part is over:

1. Don't immediately find someone else to date at the same office. You will appear insecure, shallow, and immature.
2. After a breakup, there is a real sense of vulnerability when you know that the office will be gossiping about it. But don't break down in a show of emotion or cause a scene. Decide what you will need to maintain your control and maturity, and then follow it. It may be a two-week vacation to gain perspective or evenings filled with night courses to pursue educational interests.
3. Consider a transfer to another department if you feel constantly vulnerable and unable to perform well. But don't take a demotion to do it.
4. Don't let petty jealousies get in the way of rebuilding a new relationship with a former lover. The ability to refrain from saying anything unkind about a past relationship is tremendously impressive to coworkers.

Handling an Affair When You Are Not Involved

Helen B. was in a very difficult romantic dilemma several years ago. Her boss, Michael, was having an affair with two women at the same time who worked next to each other. At the end of the day, Michael would walk either into one woman's office or the other's for an evening together. He made it even more grim because he would never commit to either one which he would see that night.

Each woman would be certain to be in her office by 5:00 P.M., even if it meant cutting an important meeting short, just to make sure she would be available. The tension between the two women who worked together and knowingly competed for this man made the office environment almost unbearable and the rest of the staff demoralized. There were daily outbursts of tears from one or the other, often over a matter that was directly related to this stressful affair.

Helen realized that she had three choices: talk to Michael, talk to her coworkers Lee and Barb, or quit. She decided that the safest path was to discuss the situation with Lee, because she was closest to her. But Lee was so emotionally involved with Michael that Helen's advice went in one ear and out the other.

Helen felt that she had pursued every avenue of recourse and had given the situation almost a year to resolve itself. Her only other course was to go to the board members of the company, who had been longtime friends with Michael. She decided against approaching them.

So in desperation, she dusted off her resume, updated it, and found another job. Subsequently three other very bright people left the organization purely because of this mishandled, emotionally destructive, and very unprofessional office romance. It took several years before the department got back on track because of the talent drain.

What's Love Got to Do with It?

Discussing someone's love affair at the office is infinitely more interesting than auditing last month's sales transactions. The higher up and the more visible in the organization the involved people are, the more they can count on being endlessly discussed by everyone below them.

Sometimes the press even gets involved, such as in the Bendix Corporation case where Mary Cunningham ended up leaving Bendix after intense pressure from the company and a constant spotlight from the newspapers. Ms. Cunningham ended up marrying her boss and moving forward with her life, despite the intense scrutiny. The situation at Calvin Klein with the principal of the company and an employee is another example of a personal romance that found its way into the front page, no doubt with distortions.

When a romance springs up at the office, the first rule is not to gossip about it. More than in any other area, no one has firsthand knowledge about someone else's love affair. Don't contribute anything even if you know what is going on. Also, by not gossiping, you won't get the reputation for being the source of all the sordid office information. Don't casually bring up the relationship with the involved persons, especially if they are senior to you. It is political suicide.

> When a romance springs up at the office, the first rule is not to gossip about it. More than in any other area, no one has first-hand knowledge about someone else's love affair.

If you are sandwiched in between an affair (your boss is dating someone who works for you) and you feel squeezed, call a meeting with your boss and discuss the situation professionally. Don't say anything that will discredit your boss's good judgment. You may decide not to bring up the romantic angle, just the fact that you are not able to do your job well because you are not getting the support from a specific staff member. A genuine sense of resentment will develop if your authority is being undermined by the affair, especially when it comes from someone who reports to you.

Never stoop to personal attacks, even if you feel they are justified. "She is such a fool. He will never leave his wife." Or "He is such a lecher, I don't know what she sees in him anyway, except for his money, of course." Throwing dirt will only cause you to lose ground. Also, if you appear to be noncommittal and nonjudgmental throughout the affair, you will win points from both parties and from the office staff, too.

Don't become the constant sounding board for one of the involved parties. When the affair is over, you will look very aligned to one party, and it could put you in an awkward position. Sometimes it is better not to have too much information.

The Case of the Newlyweds

One of our clients told us that the most disruptive romance in her career was between two married people . . . who were married to each other! Her coworker was so starry-eyed, so totally emotionally invested in her new husband that nothing got done in the office.

Between flower deliveries, balloon deliveries, intimate phone calls, lunch and dinner reservations, and a regular polling of the office staff on the best vacation spots, the entire day seemed to be devoted to love.

Everyone agreed that a secret, torrid affair would have been much more amenable to the office staff, because then some work would get done. With everything so public, with long, passionate kisses twice a day in the reception area in front of clients, everyone wished they would just knock it off and get back to business.

Finally the woman's boss simply sat her down and told her that although everyone wished her happiness in her marriage, all the time that was being taken away from the business was demoralizing to her coworkers and staff. She apologized and shaped up.

Don't Throw Bouquets at Me

The healthiest way to approach a romance with a coworker is to first determine if the affair has the potential to create mutual happiness and some level of commitment. If it doesn't, then the risk is probably too great. A mere dalliance in love may prove too complicating for the office.

If the relationship is worth continuing, these are the easiest romances to maintain:

- Single dating single
- Consenting and discreet
- Similar levels but different departments

Departing from any one of these three characteristics will not necessarily doom a relationship, but it is certain to cause more headaches and heartaches.

thirteen

Damage Control: Managing Critical Circumstances and Sticky Situations

Show no signs of choler, but do it with sweetness and mildness.

—*Manners, Culture and Dress, 1890*

Embarrassing moments that happen in the course of a workday compromise our sense of confidence and our sense of self. When we have appeared ridiculous, misspoken, or turned a minor issue into a major conflict, revisiting those occasions can still make us cringe even months or years later. Embarrassment will often cause us to avoid important contacts, clients, or associates because they were present when we made a particular faux pas. However, when we react to an embarrassing situation with grace and humility we not only can avoid further damage to our image, we may actually be able to enhance it.

Helen Neetle, an office manager with a growing firm, experienced a very sticky business situation. She was new in her city and new in her job as the office manager and supervisor for her firm—a job that promised an opportunity for future advancement. A member of a military family, she prided herself on being very organized and capable, arriving at work before 7:30 A.M. and often staying late.

As office manager, she made certain that no one except employees and clients parked in the company parking lot, because the firm's downtown location was inviting to freeloaders who wanted to avoid paying for parking. Normally, she relied on a lot attendant, but on one particular Friday he was out sick.

> When former president George Bush was in Japan at a state dinner with the prime minister, he became ill and was unable to get to the restroom so he threw up on his host. Photos of the incident appeared around the world. President Bush used humor, grace, and a sincere apology to recover.

Ever conscientious, Helen spent part of that day patrolling the lot. She immediately noticed a late-model Mercedes that she was certain didn't belong to anyone who worked in the building, nor was it registered as a client's car. After her second pass through the lot, she called the towing company and had the car removed. Thirty minutes after the tow truck pulled away from the building with the car, an irate man stormed into the reception area asserting that his car had been stolen. "Oh, no," the receptionist replied. "It was towed from our lot less than an hour ago."

Two minutes later, Helen, summoned by her boss, confidently swept into his office, only to find the CEO in a slow boil along with his angry client. They demanded an explanation about the towed vehicle. Helen was quickly made aware that the automobile she had had towed belonged to the company's most important client, who had been in an extended off-site meeting with Helen's boss.

Stunned, Helen turned scarlet and began to hyperventilate. Her body language changed from her usual large, sweeping, confident gestures, to closed, tiny movements, and she averted eye contact. She drew her arms and head into her body like a turtle defending itself and clung to the nearest doorknob. Without voicing an apology to the client, she mumbled something about checking on the situation and went straight to her office where she called the receptionist with instructions on how to retrieve the client's car. Then she hung up the telephone, grabbed her purse, and fled through the back exit.

Why this sudden metamorphosis from a confident, self-assured woman to a cringing coward? Because nothing saps our self-confidence, impacts our body language, or stymies our effectiveness quite like being the brunt of a humiliating experience.

Helen made a bad situation worse when her embarrassment made her inept. Not only did she lose control of her verbal skills and offer no apology, but her nonverbal communication said that she was totally unable to handle the consequences of her mistake.

Essentially she "said," through her presence, that she wished to shrink and disappear. She left her boss in the throes of a most unpleasant situation that he did not create, and she inconvenienced an innocent client.

Facing the Music

What could she have done? First of all, never try to defend the indefensible. Helen could have accepted full responsibility for the mistake, and she could have made sure that no one else was blamed or implicated.

She could have kept her presence calm and professional, showing she was still in control of this unfortunate occurrence. Eye contact that spoke a sincere apology and sympathetic, understanding body language would have gained her a lot of points.

Continuing the recovery, she could have listened well, empathized, and offered an immediate plan to provide the client with transportation. Also maintaining a respectful distance of three to six feet shows an awareness of the other person's personal space and anger. Staying oriented to the client's emotional needs first and then addressing the practical needs creates the best solution.

She could have clearly explained the situation: "I am so very sorry. I'm afraid I was being overzealous about our parking lot. The attendant is ill today and I just didn't recognize your car."

She also could have done whatever was necessary to rectify the situation, such as ordering a limousine for the client while she retrieved his car. The next day, sincere notes or phone calls, both to the client and her boss, would have put her apology on the record. When things cooled down and there was more perspective on the incident, she might try a little humor and creativity. A toy tow truck with a small gold plaque attached with the inscription, "To commemorate a most unfortunate incident on November 18," could have helped turn a disaster into an opportunity to show some humanness and imagination.

As it was, Helen slunk back to work the next day, kept her door closed for the rest of the week, and felt ashamed, embarrassed, and inept.

> When you learn of a serious problem, don't try to hide it. And go to your supervisor prepared with a solution. Even if it's not the solution that's selected, at least you've thought about the situation. Whatever you do, don't be paralyzed by inaction. Things will only get worse.
> —Pauli Brandt, Manager, Marketing Communications, IKON Office Solutions

An Offer They Could Refuse

One of our independent consultants spoke to a group of lawyers who were evaluating her professional image program for use in their law firm. When she finished the presentation that showed how their firm would benefit from her services, most of the partners were smiling and nodding their heads, and everyone appeared to be in general agreement. She assured them that her program would probably be a refresher for the senior partners but that with the advent of "business casual" along with a generally more casual approach to business, the newer and younger associates would receive a great deal of benefit.

However, the senior partner, the one whose name appeared first on the door, peered at her over the top of his reading glasses. In a most condescending tone, he proceeded to inform her that her program was something that parents, universities, and social exposure should have instilled. Certainly by the time one has become a lawyer with a large firm, these items of image are second nature. Eye contact, demeanor, moving with authority, and especially issues of clothing were too basic to warrant serious discussion.

Immediately, the nods of agreement ceased. The entire mood of the group went from positive to negative in about twelve seconds.

There was no point in debating this issue because the senior partner was rising to his feet, and the meeting was over.

She felt embarrassed and slightly humiliated. No one likes to be summarily dismissed, especially in front of a group. But she kept her composure, shook hands, smiled, and thanked them for their time. She kept telling herself that everyone who has stepped up to bat has struck out.

With the meeting over, she and the senior partner headed to the restrooms at the same time. A few minutes later the situation was still strained as they both awkwardly entered the elevator on the twentieth floor. Suddenly she noticed that, unknown to him, his fly was open.

Since it was almost noon, the elevator stopped on each of the top ten floors, filling up steadily and forcing everyone closer together. As they stood packed in the elevator, a women's fluffy looped bouclé jacket caught on the senior partner's open zipper.

> Most of us can think of many brilliant ways to handle an embarrassing situation once it is over.

At that point he recognized that he had a problem, but he just stood there frozen and red-faced, at a loss about what to do. His fine breeding wasn't coming up with any answers. When the elevator reached the lobby, the woman shot out of the elevator, temporarily dragging her most unwilling partner behind her as he frantically tried to disengage himself from her jacket.

Handling Embarrassment

Most of us can think of many brilliant ways to handle an embarrassing situation once it is over. But to have the necessary presence of mind when the incident occurs is a learned skill.

The unfortunate senior partner could have spent the elevator time, once he realized that he was caught in someone's jacket, in either getting himself untangled or thinking of something hilarious to say.

Humor, especially self-deprecating humor, is often the best way to recover from an embarrassing moment. But when you simply can't think of anything funny to say, be friendly and straightforward. He could have tapped her on the shoulder and said with a smile, "Excuse me, miss, but would you hold still for just a moment? I seem to be caught on your jacket."

Putting Yourself and Others at Ease

An important characteristic of presence is the ability to put others at ease while appearing comfortable yourself. Most people don't enjoy seeing someone else uncomfortable. They want the situation to return to normal as soon as possible.

When the situation warrants it, offer a sincere apology. If you drop a fork full of eggroll with duck sauce on the boss's oriental rug at a cocktail party, for example, humor would be inappropriate. In a case like this, if you can rectify the problem immediately, do so. If not, offer to have it corrected later. Fussing and over-apologizing will make everyone feel uneasy and undermine all the goodwill that is being created by the occasion.

> Fussing and over-apologizing will make everyone feel uneasy and undermine all the goodwill that is being created by the occasion.

By all means, even if no one saw you spill your coffee or break a wineglass, mention it to the proper person so that the stain can be treated or the broken glass swept up. If you accidentally spill a soda on a client's copier, for example, tell someone immediately to avoid potential damage both to the equipment and the relationship.

If you drop your briefcase on your foot and it spills open, recover as smoothly as possible. Don't stop in mid-sentence and scramble around putting papers in order, acting horrified that you could be such a klutz. Try not to make your embarrassing moments embarrassing for everyone else, too.

In a case such as this one, finish your sentence, stay relaxed with your body language, and calmly kneel down and reassemble things. If the situation can wait to be cleaned up, wait. Never add to the confusion unless absolutely necessary.

Reacting to Someone Else's Embarrassment

When another person is embarrassed, try to alleviate that individual's embarrassment. Ignore the incident, brush it off as unimportant, and if possible, help the person to recover.

In many cases, you can do a great deal to alleviate someone else's difficulty, and gain a new friend. If a client knocks over a glass of water at a working lunch and the contents spill all over your report, try not to overreact. Immediate assurance that everything is all right and can be easily replaced is a demonstration of elegant behavior.

Sometimes it helps an embarrassed person's feelings if you relate a (preferably amusing) story about a time when you were embarrassed. You might say: "Don't feel bad. You should have seen me when I ordered iced tea with lemon. As I absent-mindedly squeezed the lemon, it flew up in the air and landed on top of my head!"

It's a Bird, It's a Plane, It's . . .

One of our clients recalled a very embarrassing incident. She called on a partner with one of the big accounting firms. She admitted that she was intimidated by this executive who had 25 years as an extremely successful merger and acquisitions manager. He had put together some very impressive deals and was frequently quoted in the city's business section. He made it clear to her that he was doing her a favor . . . which he was.

Image-wise, he was extremely "together" with a custom-made Oxxford wool suit, 100% Egyptian cotton shirt, Hermés silk tie, and Bally shoes. The keys to his Mercedes sports car were visible and so was the athletic bag behind his desk. A large framed photograph of his very attractive family vacationing in the Caribbean rested on his impressive desk. He was Superman.

One of our clients, David Zarzour, attended the first dinner party of a newly wed couple 15 years ago. As the guests drank from the new couple's set of eight leaded crystal goblets, David accidentally bumped into another guest and broke his goblet. The new bride turned white, then regained her composure. She quickly and unobtrusively cleaned up the broken glass, ignored all the jokes being directed to David, washed out her goblet, filled it back up, and with her warmest smile, handed it to him. Her graciousness was remembered and acknowledged by David and every guest even 15 years following the incident.

He had everything—including a porcelain tooth that came flying out of his mouth in mid-conversation and landed on her file folder. He was absolutely mortified, and she didn't know what to do. No one had ever taught her the proper way to return someone's tooth in a casual, "This is not at all a big deal" manner.

They sat there for a while in silence. Then she picked up his tooth and carefully put it on his desk next to his golf trophy and started a conversation about golf clubs, never referring to the incident in any way.

> A golden rule of professional presence is never to make the embarrassment greater than it already is.

He, however, never really recovered, partly because of his embarrassment and partly because he didn't want to continue talking with a big gap in the front of his mouth.

He would have been better off if he had excused himself, replaced the tooth in private, and returned to continue the meeting. Or she could have indicated that she had another appointment and rescheduled with him at a later date. A golden rule of professional presence is never to make the embarrassment greater than it already is. Even turning the tables and making the incident look like your fault can be a very generous and effective gesture.

Losing Points with the Boss

In most cases, a boss is a boss—not a dear friend, not a close confidant, and not one to take lightly or flippantly. Although you may see each other daily and work closely together, certain protocol comes with this relationship.

The most obvious mistake is to criticize, in front of others, a major decision that your boss has made. You may want to select your confrontations carefully and in private.

Several years ago, we attended the launching of a new product at the annual meeting of an international cosmetics company. The new item had been in research and development for two years and was heralded as the product with the most growth potential in the entire line. After a spectacular multimedia presentation to the sales force by the president of the company, the new product was greeted with a standing ovation. But during the question-and-answer period, one of the district sales managers stood up and asked why the labeling was so confusing. He also wanted to know why such an unattractive female model was chosen for the ad campaign.

In one fell swoop, he significantly dampened the enthusiasm that the president had worked hard to create, and negated months of effort by the creative team. The other attendees began to mutter among themselves. The president abruptly cut off questions, and the meeting ended on an adverse note. The next day the district manager received an early morning phone call from his boss, saying that he was no longer needed in his position.

Unless there is an immediate remedy available, why create a no-win confrontation with the boss? Attacking the boss's decisions in public is certainly a CLM—career limiting move. Even a private discussion would have been nonproductive because this was not a planning meeting. This was a product launch where the objective was to become enthused over the new product, not to embarrass the boss.

Other issues that can create friction and may cause problems with your supervisor include:

- Ignoring an important social invitation from the boss
- Getting drunk at a company function
- Overtly flirting with a customer or colleague
- Inviting your supervisor to social events with your close personal friends
- Back slapping, arm grabbing, and other physical contact other than a handshake
- Insisting on discussing business in a purely social situation
- Ignoring their spouse or children
- Not deferring seating to him or her in a meeting
- Expecting the boss to lug around the heavy equipment or the luggage on a business trip
- Wasting the boss's time with frequent tales of your many personal problems

Positioning yourself professionally with your boss and others up the ladder means that you will come to mind when opportunities and special projects come up. Good supervisors know which employees to keep in the background and which to trust in visible positions. Those with presence, people skills, and good communication are repeatedly tapped because they know what to do as well as what not to do.

> Companies, just like high schools, have both team players and troublemakers.

If you are unfortunate enough to have a selfish, immature, or just inept boss, as everyone has had at one time or another, it is still to your professional and personal advantage to afford your boss a level of respect. Not responding to every slight and at times defending your supervisor's position when it makes sense will not detract from your personal or professional strength.

If, for example, you are forced to listen to a litany of woes when your boss plunks down in your office, listen, don't offer advice, and then work to redirect the subject back to business.

Bad Company

Companies, just like high schools, have both team players and troublemakers. Remember the kind of student who always caused trouble, bullying others, stirring up strife, and lying to cover himself—the Eddie Haskell type from the reruns of *Leave It to Beaver*?

Malcolm Zatt is Eddie all grown up. He is competitive and can be self-destructive. Although he is above average in sales, he frequently cheats on his expense accounts when he travels, with acts as brazen as taking a load of dirty clothes with him on a trip to have them cleaned at the company's expense.

He loves to take on the boss in staff meetings, seemingly for the sake of argument, and he never misses a chance to point out a colleague's error, making sure that everyone else hears him. During meetings when others are presenting, he opens up his laptop and spends his time checking e-mail and working on his latest report. The problem is that Malcolm has taken a liking to Thomas Wiggins, a rather quiet, hard-working product manager.

Malcolm invariably sits by Tom in meetings, making sarcastic comments under his breath and elbowing Tom when he wants to call attention to someone's blunder. The staff resents Malcolm, and they are unfortunately beginning to think of Malcolm and Tom as a team.

Tom realizes that Malcolm's reputation is rubbing off on him, but he doesn't know how to terminate the relationship without making Malcolm angry. Although Tom doesn't want him for an enemy, it's more risky to continue the friendship.

Friendships develop naturally when people work together. Sharing a meal, asking for another point of view on a problem, and actively teaming up with good people is part of professional growth. But when you sense that the association is going to be a bad one, like the Malcolm/Tom relationship, then it is time to decline lunch, tactfully stay busy every night after work, and seat yourself between two other people at meetings. Sooner or later the other person will get the message.

Turning Negatives into Positives

Professional presence is never more important than when it sees us through both critical circumstances and sticky situations. The way we behave under difficult circumstances can actually cause us to emerge in a better position than had the incident never occurred. When other people see us handle ourselves well under stress, they become aware of an added dimension. We aren't just a business façade; we display some depth.

Businesspeople have a universal admiration for those who are clear, focused, and proactive when under the gun. We read books about them and listen to them speak to gain more understanding of the qualities that have made them successful. Most of us see that true character reveals itself only under

> When we have the presence to behave well and decently when things are falling apart, we will certainly emerge even more strongly under normal business conditions.

pressure. It's easy to be effective and successful when there are no adversities.

When we have the presence to behave well and decently when things are falling apart, we will certainly emerge even more strongly under normal business conditions.

Most situations are repairable. Whether we have called unfavorable attention to ourselves or embarrassed our boss, the way we recover and repair the incident will say a great deal about our character and abilities. No one goes through a career without making blunders. Work to keep these occurrences in perspective.

fourteen 14

Business Travel: Navigating Etiquette on the Road

There are a sufficient number of discomforts in traveling, at best, and it should be the aim of each passenger to lessen them as much as possible, and to cheerfully bear his own part. Life is a journey, and we are all fellow-travelers.

—Manners, Culture and Dress, 1890

You are at the end of a four-city business trip and heading home on Friday, anxious to go attend your son's soccer game and play golf with your regular foursome. Your flight is delayed twice, first by weather, now by a mechanical "difficulty." After patiently sitting in your seat for 45 minutes on the ground, you have just been informed that you must change planes.

You collect your papers, stuff them into your briefcase, and tiredly make your way, along with the rest of the passengers, to the designated gate. As you elbow your way aboard the new plane, it is clear that your originally assigned bulkhead seat has been taken. A weary-looking woman holding a baby with a five-year-old girl seated beside her now occupies it. You don't have the heart to ask them to move.

You ask the harried flight attendant for help and she points to the last seat in coach. You are now wedged between a teenager with her Sony Walkman and a chatty older man who is delighted that you

181

haven't tuned him out with earphones so that you two can become "really good friends."

Is traveling worth the trouble? Can we maintain a powerful professional presence on the road? Of course!

The Travel Advantage

As effective as the telephone is, it will never replace the reassurance of a personal meeting between a buyer and a salesperson, a patient and a doctor, a stockbroker and a client. Lyndon Johnson, even in ill health, insisted on a face-to-face meeting with the Vietnamese in Hawaii. Signed documents, phone calls, and assurances by top-level officials aren't as conclusive as the power of a personal meeting.

> Many people get their best ideas while traveling.

Many people get their best ideas while traveling. Their energy flows, and their creative juices get a jolt from new faces and new places. Traveling can be energizing and can clear out the cobwebs.

Several presidents of companies with whom we work have confided that they often attend out-of-town trade shows or conventions, routinely visit regional offices, or teach a class at a university in another state just so that they can have a day to break the routine of their office work and think more creatively. Traveling rejuvenates their imagination and gives them a fresh perspective.

Often, associates will have almost unlimited access to their boss during road trips. This kind of uninterrupted time can be invaluable. Gripes can be aired and thoroughly discussed, industry gossip and ideas can be exchanged, and helpful information can be passed on in an environment with much less time constraint than on the telephone or at a sales meeting.

Business relationships can be cemented by travel because the relationship becomes multidimensional and often more personal. Your boss's passion for estate sales and antiques may never have surfaced at the office but will become an important link to a closer relationship with you when it is discussed at length over an unhurried, out-of-town dinner. If you enjoy traveling with your boss, tell him or her; it is a genuine compliment. If you don't enjoy the company, then reschedule your trip either prior to or after their flight and plan only one dinner together.

Getting There and Doing the Job

Business travel, despite its benefits, can be long on stress. It can erode the composure and presence that are much easier to maintain on our own home turf. Whatever method you use to travel, the effort of getting there is sometimes more work than the actual labor of transacting business.

One client, who recently started traveling as a consulting engineer, said that she was exhausted by the time she finally arrived in her designated city and just wanted to head to the hotel and sleep. She felt she had done her job for that day just by traveling six hours. "Travel is work enough. I dragged my luggage from the plane to the metro to the cab. I can't imagine that I will ever have the stamina to see clients, too!"

> In business travel, try changing the pace and relaxing.

It does take stamina, as well as grace and a sense of humor, to be a productive business traveler. You may love traveling, hate it, or simply tolerate it, but until we have the technology to "Beam us up, Scotty," face-to-face encounters requiring travel will continue to be the best environment for doing business.

One problem is that businesspeople often overschedule their travel so that by the time they arrive at the important meeting, they have lost a great deal of their effectiveness due to being stressed out. Overeating and overdrinking will wear out even the strongest person. Running on all eight cylinders on the road means that you might be burned out and broken down when you get back to the home office. If a meeting is important, allow an extra night to rest.

In business travel, try changing the pace and relaxing. For instance, instead of eating a huge, fattening meal that probably would get in the way of a good night's sleep, opt for a relaxing massage or a light workout instead. Most hotels have health clubs or exercise facilities. Large hotels typically offer spa services.

If you have the time, see a play. Most people don't think about the theater unless they are in New York City. There are usually fine performances in all cities, and often single tickets are available 30 minutes before the performance. Opera, classical concerts, and rock concerts can also be a real treat. Losing yourself in a live performance is a wonderful way to de-stress and rejuvenate. If you and your significant other differ in your preference of movies, this is the time to see what you like.

It can be fun to get a manicure or pedicure, too. Just don't try a haircut or hair color out of town, unless you have a strong personal recommendation from someone you really trust. Don't let the intrigue of new surroundings cloud your good judgment.

The Graceful Traveler

Those who possess presence have mastered the art of being a graceful traveler; they seldom complain about the unavoidable difficulties and delays of travel. They also know when it's possible to change circumstances by complaining successfully and when to remain quiet and make the best of things. They have a sense of priority, of knowing what is really important, which gives them added power over their circumstances.

Handling delays with grace is part of having professional presence.

It's obvious that no airline, bus service, or rental company wants to delay passengers. This is expensive both in terms of money and loss of customer loyalty. So, although you have a right to get straight answers, yelling at the employees usually doesn't accomplish anything.

Handling delays with grace is part of having professional presence. In the airport you can always retreat to an airline club and make phone calls, read a report, or watch television. In other locations, you can buy some ice cream, get a paperback novel, or catch up on your business reading.

Keeping Comfortable Aloft

Although trains have certainly made a comeback for pleasure travel and buses are favored by John Madden and Cher, the majority of business travelers get to where they need to go by car or plane. Let's take a look at some airline issues first.

The more relaxed you are in your travels, the more impressive you will be when you arrive. Long airline flights will not seem as grueling if you exercise. Walk to the restroom and just stand near the door. You could even read a magazine, or flip through a report, while stretching. If someone starts to queue up behind you, just wave them past and continue your reading and leg stretching.

Do isometric exercises in your seat. Start with your toes, curling and uncurling them, and work up. Move to the balls of your foot and back on the heel. Press palms together and release. Roll your shoulders forward and backward. Circle your head. Getting your circulation and muscles moving will make the trip more tolerable, and you will experience less jet lag at the other end.

> If you inadvertently disturb or offend someone, then handle the incident as diplomatically as possible. And always apologize. A sincere "I am so sorry" goes a long way.

If the issue is one that you prefer not to address directly, inform the flight attendant. Although that option may feel like squealing to the teacher in class, it is usually better to quietly address any major grievance to a flight attendant. For instance, if a passenger has an offensive odor, you probably aren't the only one complaining. If someone is loud and drunk, everyone will be affected. Even for a relatively minor issue, such as being too hot or too cold, inform the attendant.

If you inadvertently disturb or offend someone, then handle the incident as diplomatically as possible. And always apologize. A sincere "I am so sorry" goes a long way.

Arm Wrestling and Other Airline Games

Armrest etiquette, as simple as it seems, can generate bad feelings on an airplane. If you end up in the center seat and the other two passengers have claimed both armrests, you will be left like a sardine in the middle, feeling resentful.

The proper etiquette is that the middle person, being more squeezed and inconvenienced, gets two armrests. The other two passengers each get one armrest because one has the window for a sense of space, and the other has the added space of the aisle.

Patience and goodwill can minimize difficulties. The mother with the baby, bogged down with all the appropriate gear, and the elderly person who has difficulty getting to his or her seat are often the victims of scowls and impatient gestures from fellow travelers.

Such scenes are repeated hundreds of times each day, although the elderly person could just as well be a silk-suited businesswoman, and the parent, a harried father. It's not fair to blame a parent for having a child that needs to be on your flight. Traveling families are a fact of life.

> It's not fair to blame a parent for having a child that needs to be on your flight. Traveling families are a fact of life.

More appropriate behavior is to sit down, and acknowledge the parent and child. After the plane takes off, murmur your apologies about having to do a report and look for another seat. Or quietly ask the flight attendant if someone with a child would want to trade. Never harangue the parent, frown at the child, or give the cold shoulder. Being accidentally kicked, hit by flying Play-Doh, being wailed at by an unhappy child, are experiences we've all had, but we're still here to talk about it. No parent wants an unhappy camper on a crowded airplane, but infants and very young children simply can't be switched on and off for the comfort of others.

Eating and Drinking in Flight

Having someone crunch popcorn or pretzels in your ear certainly isn't pleasant. If you are ravenous, try to eat before you get on the plane. If you do bring food on, select only neatly eaten food—no ice cream bars with the chocolate dripping off the sides—and try to eat your food when other meals are being served. Your snack shouldn't be overly messy or too fragrant. A Limburger cheese and onion sandwich, for example, would probably find you sitting alone.

The best advice in terms of liquor is not to drink at all. But if you do, limit your drinks to one on short flights and two on longer ones. If you travel frequently between the same cities, chances are you may run into clients, coworkers, or the competition. There is no point in ruining your presence by appearing a little too tipsy.

If you don't drink, you will arrive much more refreshed and suffer less from jet lag. But if the liquor is free, which it always is in first class, and often is if the plane takes off late, then the temptation is usually too great. Even drinks in coach are very reasonable and can take the edge off a long trip. Just remember that one drink in the air is the equivalent of two on the ground, and if you love to talk, you will definitely become more loquacious with your seatmates.

Ten Tips for Packing Smart

1. Pack as light as possible. On overnight trips, organize your garments so you can bring your luggage on the plane. With either long or short trips, anticipate your activities. Decide what garments will be required and make a list. Sometimes it is as easy as taking three strong business outfits and one fuzzball-covered sweatsuit with no requirements for anything else. Women should pick one primary color, like black, so that a minimum of accessories will be needed. For a week-long trip, pack two suits and wear the third one. For fewer wrinkles during the trip, a woman can turn her skirt around and sit on the front of it. Then when she arrives, she can readjust her skirt with virtually no wrinkles in the front and her jacket hiding the ones in the back.

   > Darker garments are safer because dirt, spots, and stains are much less apparent on a navy suit than on a khaki one.

   For long trips involving lengthy travel time, wear comfortable clothes and pack all three suits. Darker garments are safer because dirt, spots, and stains are much less apparent on a navy suit than on a khaki one.

2. Don't pack a bathrobe. It takes up too much room and many hotels provide them.

3. If you exercise, bring the minimum amount of exercise gear. Leotards or running shorts are easy to pack. Swimming is great because it requires so little in the way of apparatus, but be sure to bring plastic bags in case you have to pack a wet suit. Insert athletic shoes into old woolen socks or wrap in plastic dry-cleaning bags to make sure they don't get anything else dirty.

4. Pack one pair of dark, comfortable business shoes and wear a second pair of business shoes. Rotating two pairs is much more comfortable. They can be polished at the airport or hotel. Both men and women should go for comfort. Never bring a new pair of shoes on a trip.

5. Don't bother bringing a travel iron or a hair dryer. Even economy hotels will supply them if you call ahead. But do include a small, collapsible umbrella.

6. Select suits and blouses that need a minimum of pressing on arrival, or better yet, don't need to be pressed at all. Expensive silk or wool doesn't wrinkle much. Inexpensive silk or wool wrinkles greatly. Purchase a tie case to keep ties smooth and clean.

To further minimize wrinkling, try these ideas:
- Wrap easily wrinkled items in tissue paper or plastic dry-cleaning bags.
- Keep the plastic dry-cleaning bags intact on suits and then pack everything into a garment bag.
- Bring a can of "wrinkle-free" spray.
- Ask for a cardboard garment box at airport check-in for soft-sided luggage or garment bags. Most are sturdy so they can be recycled for future trips.

7. If you travel a great deal, have duplicate cosmetic items. Keep your travel shampoo, shaver, shaving cream, mascara, blush,

eye shadow, and anything else you need in a separate cosmetic bag or travel kit that never gets used at home. It makes it a breeze to pack because everything is prepacked.

8. For peace of mind, take along expensive jewelry only if it can be worn all the time. Watches, rings, earrings, and bracelets that work with your travel wardrobe are fine. Cuff links can be easily lost or stolen. Hotel rooms are not safe places to store valuables. Put jewelry in your carry-on baggage, not in checked luggage.

9. Purchase luggage that won't embarrass you when you lift it off the conveyer belt or bring it into a hotel. It's just as important as your briefcase or handbag.

10. Be sure to put identification tags on everything. A business address is safer than a home one. Don't waste time at the airport filling them out. Have them already attached. Even carry-on bags should have a luggage tag. If you have ever left a briefcase at a pay phone, you will understand the wisdom of identifying everything.

Tips on Tipping While Traveling

Nothing is more embarrassing than having only a $50 bill when you need a $2 tip. Keep a roll of at least ten $1 bills in a convenient pocket for quick, discreet tipping.

In a hotel, tip a dollar per bag. If the bellperson has provided unusual service like getting ice, spending 10 minutes telling you about the best restaurants in town, or arranging for an iron and ironing board to be brought up immediately, you might want to increase the tip.

You can save on tipping at the airport if you bring your own bags inside. Otherwise, at curbside the appropriate tip is $1 for each bag. If you are late for your flight, wave a $5 bill for more immediate service and tell the skycap to expedite your luggage.

Cab drivers generally receive between 10 and 15 percent of the fare depending on their politeness, how carefully they drove, and the cleanliness of their cabs. If your cab ride lacks these amenities, just pay the fare.

A Clean Car Is a Blissful Car

If driving is your preference and you will be using your vehicle to transport others, make sure your car stays both clean and organized. Not many people would bring their customers or clients into a home with trash on the floor, with visibly smudged windows, or candy-bar wrappers stuffed between the seats of the couch. But they don't seem to give a second thought to driving customers around in a grubby car.

Research has indicated that people feel depressed when they drive a dirty car. It is hard to perform professionally when the steering wheel is greasy from French fries, or mud from a camping trip is still on the carpet, or you have to sift through piles of old newspapers on the floor to find your account book.

If you drive for a business, you will be rewarded for having a clean car. A spotless automobile makes a great first impression when you are taking clients out to dine or just picking them up at the airport. One of our clients who is a sales manager can't count the number of times that someone has greeted him at the airport, and almost before saying hello, has blurted out, "My car is a real mess and I never got around to cleaning it. Sorry!"

Even if you don't carry others in your car, the personal benefit of having a clean car is worth the trouble it takes to clean it. You feel organized, clean, and efficient. You can also feel assured that there's no risk of sitting on a leftover tuna fish sandwich and ruining your suit.

Romance on the Road

Never invite a client or customer back to your hotel room. It simply isn't worth the risk of being misunderstood. If they need to get something that is in your room, ask them to wait in the lobby or have the bellperson deliver it to their room.

One saleswoman innocently went back to a salesman's room to get some samples for a training session held the next morning. As he was digging around in his sample case, his phone rang and without thinking, he asked her to grab it. It was his wife, who wasn't too thrilled that a woman was answering his phone at 10:00 at night. She icily asked for her husband.

It was embarrassing for the saleswoman, humiliating for the salesman, and infuriating for the spouse. Also, why risk the implication if a coworker sees you leave someone else's room at a late hour if other arrangements can be made?

> Affairs of the heart on the road are not only dangerous but may also be an assault on a business reputation.

You also never really know when something can come back to haunt you. Twelve businesspeople had arrived to a meeting by plane from different parts of the country. Unknowingly, two of the attendees sat beside each other on a flight. Brian made pretty clear advances toward Michelle after 10 minutes of conversation. She quickly refused them and they didn't speak much during the rest of the flight. He was mortified when he saw Michelle entering the same session he was attending the next morning. Affairs of the heart on the road are not only dangerous but may also be an assault on a business reputation. They may provide temporary distraction, but they can end up creating a great deal more stress.

More Pointers from Seasoned Travelers

If you have access to a helicopter, private jet, and chauffeur-driven limousine, plus an entourage of minions to plan your personal itinerary, maximum travel efficiency would be assured. Unfortunately, this is not the reality for most of us who must travel.

Clients cancel out, appointments get changed, and colleagues fail to show up at the airport. Unexpected things do happen. Illness, family problems, and other urgent business cannot be planned. Therefore, confirm and reconfirm appointments and flight times to maximize your business travel. Never set up an appointment and assume it stands. Follow up with an e-mail, a fax, or a letter, and at least one phone call, which should be in the afternoon prior to your travel day.

Confirming plans accomplishes two things. One, the date and place are clearly established. Two, you position your time as limited and your presence as valuable. With follow up, 99 percent of scheduled meetings will happen as planned.

> Don't have major arguments over the phone with people in the office.

Unless you are in a business that has a lot of emergencies, don't check back with your office more than twice a day. It eats up a lot of time, and most situations can wait until you are less pressured.

Don't have major arguments over the phone with people in the office. When feeling out of control because of distance, the situation is usually exacerbated. Do damage control and then wait until you are back at the office to really effect a solution.

Ten Specific Ideas for Business Travel

1. Bring a laptop computer, business stationery, and envelopes in a large envelope. Quick agreements can be executed and important letters sent immediately.
2. Travel with at least one granola bar or emergency snack.
3. Make sure at least two people from your office, plus your family, have your hotel phone number.
4. Keep an emergency first-aid kit in your briefcase. Sixty-two percent of all business travelers suffered from some physical ailment in the past year. It is hard to have power and professional presence when you are suffering from an upset stomach, headache, indigestion, a cold, or a cough.
5. Never dress shabbily for a flight. You never know whom you will meet on the plane.
6. You are responsible for the total area that you create with your belongings. Watch how you swing that hanging bag or bulky shoulder luggage as you walk down the aisle. Clipping the head of a fellow passenger, though unintentional, is rude.

7. In most cases, be sure your last appointment knows your departure schedule. However, if you are in serious negotiations, don't give away your departure time.

8. Bring along a framed picture of your favorite person, dog, or cat for your hotel room. It will bring warmth and connection to you after a long day.

9. Order flowers, fruit, or a plate of homemade cookies through the hotel to welcome an out-of-town customer. This kind of thoughtfulness makes a wonderful impression. If you feel entitled to it, order the same for yourself if you have had a weary flight.

10. Bring one stretched-out, worn-out, and totally comfortable T-shirt and pants for relaxing. This is the perfect outfit to wear at the end of a long day of business meetings when you flop on your bed, switch on an in-room movie, and order room service.

Step Five

Develop
Social Savvy

fifteen

Planning the Business Meal: Gracious, Sophisticated Manners

Nothing indicates the good breeding of a gentleman so much as his manners at table. There are a thousand little points to be observed, which, although not absolutely necessary, distinctly stamp the refined and well-bred man. A man may pass muster by dressing well, and may sustain himself tolerably in conversation; but if he be not perfectly 'au fait' dinner will betray him.

—*Manners, Culture and Dress, 1890*

The business meal has taken on all forms. A three-hour lunch at the club is a luxury, not always a reality. More realistic is a succinct breakfast at the local pancake house, a hot dog shared in the park, or a sandwich at the airport. Cocktail parties where contacts are made and formal dinners are few and far between, but the gambit of occasions to make an impression and display presence is significant. Consequently, our skill set must be expanded so that we are as comfortable in a Japanese restaurant as we are having lunch in our office. The objective is not to see how much or how often you can eat at your company's expense. The objective is to develop relationships.

A friend of ours who is a stockbroker invites clients to lunch and often orders only vichyssoise. This cold potato soup is elegant and can't cool off because it is served chilled. He usually grabs a sandwich going back to the office, but during his lunch, he has been able to focus fully on his client.

Part of developing relationships is knowing what to do and how to do it. Part of effective dining is to illustrate innate good manners. That is why it is difficult to eat like an animal at home and expect to adopt a different set of manners in public.

> Impeccable manners are meaningless if they aren't executed with confidence.
> —Elisabeth Egan, "Mind Your Manners: How to Behave at the Table"

The comfort of picking up the phone, setting up a meal, and eating together further cements a relationship. Simply put, we do business with people we know. But to create presence, a business meal must be done with style, savvy, and sophistication.

Breakfast Meetings: The Early Bird Takes Control

Breakfast is an ingenious way to build relationships. It is less expensive, both in money and in time. It fits into people's schedules more easily than do lunches and dinners. It doesn't carve into the business day. It is a peppy, energizing, and upbeat way to do business. Most businesspeople will commit to a breakfast meeting, whereas they might decline a lunch or dinner.

Hotel coffee shops or dining rooms are usually the best places to meet because they are less crowded, parking is easier, and the tables usually have tablecloths, which lends a little more elegance than cracked Formica.

Breakfast meetings are the best times to get maximum attendance. There is a certain dynamic quality to people who regularly schedule breakfast meetings. They are on the fast track and prefer to wake up an hour early to meet a client, rather than spend two hours at lunch when they could be making sales calls and working on the phone. Most power breakfasters eat lunch on the run; with breakfast they will already have satisfied their desire for a sit-down meal.

Breakfast at a fast-food restaurant is such a slice of Americana. It humanizes a corporate life on the road when we see moms, kids, and blue-collar folks. It is a quick and efficient way to meet colleagues to discuss a new project. It can also be a change of pace for a breakfast business meeting with well-established customers, and it is certainly more economical than the alternatives.

The Lunch Crunch

Lunch is still the most popular business meal, but the timing has changed. Rule number one—avoid the crunch. Try scheduling lunch at an odd hour so you won't waste time fighting the crowds, or schedule it at a restaurant that takes lunch reservations. Although only higher-priced restaurants will take reservations at midday, it is worth paying a little more for the security of knowing you won't be hanging around the lobby for 20 minutes wasting a client's time. Be sure to dine at a restaurant before you take a customer there.

> Don't talk business until everyone has looked at the menu, decided what they want, and ordered.

Try to frequent the same restaurant regularly because you will be familiar with the menu selections, the best table, the restrooms, and the telephones. You will also have had an opportunity to introduce yourself to the maître d', who will then be able to greet you on subsequent visits by name. If you can find a good restaurant that is personally managed by the proprietor, there is an added feeling of warmth, comfort, and familiarity.

If you belong to a club, you will generally be guaranteed a good table with the leisure to extend the lunch if you need to. Many clubs offer "lunch only" privileges for a much lower initiation fee.

Don't talk business until everyone has looked at the menu, decided what they want, and ordered. Otherwise you will be constantly interrupted and your effectiveness will be diminished. As the host or hostess, take charge of the lunch and instruct the waitperson when you want to order.

Your manners on view in public strongly affect your company's image as well as your own. You should be aware of the nuances of behavior whether you are acting as a host or as a guest. Even a seemingly insignificant act, such as the way you order from the waiter, can become a strong negative in others' opinion of your executive potential and presence.

—Letitia Baldridge's Complete Guide to Executive Manners

Save the most important business information for after the main entrée. Over coffee and dessert, weighty topics get more attention than between forkfuls of a roast beef platter. Time your questions so the person to whom you have asked the question won't feel embarrassed by being caught with a mouth full of food. Learn to answer a question with a bit of food in your mouth. It is exasperating to dine with someone who will speak only when they have a completely empty mouth.

Spirits at lunch is passé. In fact, ordering hard liquor at lunch creates the image of a person with a drinking problem. Wine or beer should be the "hardest" liquids at noonday.

A colleague found herself in an uncomfortable situation with a client. He was notorious for drinking at lunch and didn't appreciate the fact that she preferred not to drink with him. She ordered one vodka tonic, then excused herself to go to the ladies room. She passed the bar on the way, slid the bartender a ten dollar bill and said, "The next drink I order, make sure it's all tonic and no vodka." While most people aren't pressured to drink anymore in business, there are always exceptions. Sometimes it's not worth the time or the energy it takes to explain your personal position on alcohol when you could be focusing on building the business relationship.

Dining Leisurely

Business dinners are the most gracious way to develop a business relationship. They are generally much more leisurely than lunch, and often extend to three hours. They allow the time and opportunity to discuss much more than business. When someone enjoys your company enough to suggest dinner, you have been paid a compliment.

But there are three dangers inherent in a dinner, as opposed to breakfast, lunch, or tea. The first is the open-ended aspect of the evening meal. When does it end? The second issue is that liquor is almost always involved. The third is that dinner is the closest thing to a date without being a date, so the ambiguity can be dangerous.

The first issue can be comfortably resolved with an invitation that involves not only what time dinner is, but also a reference to the fact that the restaurant is casual and not formal. That immediately indicates that the evening won't be drawn out with various courses. You can also make a reference to your client's tight schedule or acknowledge the need to get home to his or her family and promise an early evening.

Dinner is different from lunch. It's more of a social event. It is very difficult to relax, exchange family anecdotes and fishing tips, and then hit a client with a price increase. If you have weighty business issues to discuss, try to do it at the bar or in the dining room prior to dinner.

Unless you are an extremely smooth negotiator, don't try to soften a customer's defenses and then sock them with hard issues. This feels like a breach of trust. In fact, depending on the success of the dinner, you may decide to forego serious business entirely and just establish a relationship. You can always follow up with a business meeting in their office the following day.

After specific issues have been discussed, order dinner, enjoy an after-dinner coffee, but forego any bar hopping afterwards. Babysitters and early morning meetings are always viable excuses, if you really feel you need one to end an evening.

The issue of drinking can become sticky. It is always acceptable not to drink. But it is not acceptable to make someone feel uncomfortable if they enjoy drinking. With no further business commitments at the end of the day, this is the most logical time to imbibe.

One of our female clients who owns a manufacturing company has customers who love to drink, especially if she is picking up the tab. They always want to meet at the bar and it becomes a protracted and very liquid prelude to dinner.

She has solved this by quietly telling the bartender, after 30 minutes, to keep pouring drinks if they are requested, but with a minute amount of liquor. She also tries to invite her customers to restaurants other than at their hotel. They are generally more responsible in their drinking because they know they can't just stagger onto the elevator and flop into bed.

To keep a business dinner from looking like a date, spouses are sometimes invited just to make certain that the intent is clear. It is also a nice compliment to the spouse. However, the whole flavor of a meeting changes when spouses are involved and the event becomes almost purely social.

So how does a business dinner stay that way? For starters, don't hold a chair for your client. That looks and feels like a date. Ask for a quiet table, but not one in the dark. Stay away from restaurants that are traditionally enjoyed by lovers. You know the kind . . . cozy, warm, and intimate. Don't share food or drink.

> To keep a business dinner from looking like a date, spouses are sometimes invited just to make certain that the intent is clear.

One of our single male clients in California has a designated female business companion whom he invites whenever he has asked a female customer to dinner. He always tells his guest that someone from the office will be accompanying him. "I know I sound like a coward, but for me the dinner goes much smoother with my female colleague accompanying me and there is never any concern over ambiguities."

Good Advice for Any Meal

Don't spend a great deal of time scrutinizing the menu. If you have a hard time making a decision about what kind of soup you want, the question becomes, "Can this person make a decision in business?"

Don't take any medication in front of clients, especially those for a nervous stomach, ulcer, or a headache. If you need to take medicine, excuse yourself or wait until they excuse themselves.

Don't be overly conversational with the waitperson. Be friendly and polite, but diffusing the attention from your client to the person delivering your food is not good form.

Don't select exactly the same thing that a new client orders. It may look obsequious. At least order a different salad dressing, vegetable, or dessert. Although it is usually flattering for clients to see that you share the same tastes in food, be careful that at the first dining experience together, you don't appear like a sycophant.

Don't order soup unless you can eat it quietly and without spilling. Don't order pasta, triple-decker BLTs, huge, juicy hamburgers, corn on the cob, or anything that is eaten with the fingers. If a food selection cannot be attractively eaten, don't order it during a business meal.

Take command but don't present a laundry list of topics to cover that you just give cursory attention to before jumping on to the next one. The whole reason to dine together is to establish a comfortable, trusting relationship. Racing from one thing to the next doesn't build a relationship. You will look insecure and pushy.

As the host or hostess of a business meal, it is up to you to make sure that the level of service is there for everyone. Inquire as to the quality of their food, and make sure you and your guest don't get hung out to dry with slow service. As the host or hostess, you should be the one to get a missing fork, to request additional rolls or more hot coffee for your guests.

> As the host or hostess of a business meal, it is up to you to make sure that the level of service is there for everyone.

When entertaining clients, always order the same progression of food so that they won't be eating alone. If you generally don't order an appetizer and salad and the client does, then order just one of the initial courses and keep it during their appetizer and salad. If you know you will be stuffed by the time the entrée comes, or you are watching your weight, don't eat much. But at least have something in front of you. It is always awkward to eat when no one else is eating, so don't make your client feel ill at ease dining alone.

The host or hostess should always order last. Then you can take your customer's lead and order accordingly. If the guest orders liquor, the host or hostess should order something to drink, but it doesn't have to be alcoholic. If your guest declines liquor, the host or hostess generally does the same.

When coffee is served, request the check and confirm whatever follow-up commitments will be necessary. Do check the bill quickly. Mentally do the arithmetic ahead of time so that you have some idea of the bill. If the amount is wrong, quietly excuse yourself to the front desk and discuss it out of earshot of your guests.

The word TIP comes from "To Insure Promptness." Tip money was originally placed on the table prior to a customer being served. If you want really wonderful service, tip prior to ordering, but do it so that no one sees you.

Everyone knows that tipping is optional but expected in the United States. Twenty percent for good service and a low total is appropriate. If your lunch was $5 and you received good service, leave a $1 (20 percent) tip. If your dinner tab was $300, the restaurant was casual, and you received good service, it is perfectly appropriate to leave $45 (15 percent) because of the large amount of the bill. Round off the amount to the nearest quarter (or dollar if the amount is over $50) and tip on the pretax amount.

For very formal dining the following guide is appropriate:

- $5 to $20 to the concierge or maître d' if you received an exceptional table, you want to make a favorable impression, or you received special consideration, such as getting a table when the restaurant is completely booked. Give the money in a handshake when you make a request, either as you are seated or as you leave.
- 5 percent to the captain—added into the total bill. You will recognize the captain because this is the person who takes your order, cooks tableside, and sometimes presents the bill. The captain receives only 5 percent because he supervises six to eight waiters.
- 15 percent to the waiter—added into the total bill. The waiter serves your food and beverages and attends to special requests including supervising the busboy.

- $3 to $6 to the wine steward or sommelier for each bottle of wine. If there is no room on the charge slip to add this, then it can be done with a handshake.

You can also write the dollar amount of 20 percent of the total bill over the blanks on the credit card slip where the captain's tip and the waiter's tip are. Then the service people are responsible for dividing up the amount.

Additional Tipping

- $1 to the ladies' room attendant
- $1 per coat to the coat-room attendant
- $1 to the doorman for summoning your car or getting a cab
- $1 to $2 to the parking-lot attendant. It is a great show of elegance and personal power to walk clients to their car and then tip the attendant for them. I have a female client who does this regularly for her male customers and they are always quite flattered.
- $1 per bag to the skycap checking your bags at the airport

Getting Taken for a Ride

If you extend an invitation to a client or customer, it is normally expected that you pick up the bill. However if your guest is adamant about paying for their own portion, quietly agree and just split it. The easiest way is to offer two credit cards. When entertaining guests from out of town, especially clients, the rule of thumb is "My town, my check, your town, your check."

Gender has nothing to do with who pays the bill. If you want to pay and anticipate a battle, arrive early, give your waiter your credit card imprint, and insist that they not allow your guest to pay.

If you are having lunch with colleagues, each pays for their own. If everyone generally orders the same thing, just split the bill evenly. Take charge. Pick up the bill, look at the amount, and quietly announce what each person should contribute, which should always include tax and tip. If the meals were extremely disproportionate in cost, try to take that into consideration. But if someone had an extra drink or an appetizer, just be gracious and split evenly.

Many colleagues just take turns picking up the tab. One person picks up the whole amount for one lunch, and the next lunch tab is picked up by the other. The key here is trust, knowing that your generosity will be reciprocated at a later date.

One company that we work with has an unspoken agreement with their vendors that they take turns picking up the check at the various trade show dinners. Since the tabs are usually around $600, everyone remembers who picked up the last one. Our client paid for the March show and when everyone reconvened for May, the vendors disappeared when the bill came. After three cups of after-dinner coffee the check was still on the table, and although the vendors did come back, they didn't even attempt to pick up the check.

It finally got so awkward that our client just paid the bill, but very grudgingly. He didn't want to risk losing their business, but they had violated an important rule and broken the trust that had previously been there. And sadly, the main reason for breaking bread together, which is to build relationships, had turned into bad feelings and resentment. The next time they met at a trade show, our client declined the vendors' dinner invitation. With a quick apology and an offer to host the dinner, the vendor could have repaired the relationship and gotten things back on track. Without clarity, the relationship stayed frayed and unresolved.

> If the check sits there staring at you and your meal mate, and you assumed that you were the guest, you have two options. First, you can just pick up the check and pay the whole amount. Second, you can pick up the bill, and quietly announce, "Well, why don't we split this."

If the check sits there staring at you and your meal mate, and you assumed that you were the guest, you have two options. First, you can just pick up the check and pay the whole amount. Second, you can pick up the bill, and quietly announce, "Well, why don't we split this."

Susan was asked out to lunch at a very expensive restaurant several years ago by a woman who wanted help developing her business.

She wanted her advice on the feasibility of her business, she wanted to brainstorm, and she wanted the names of clients, accountants, lawyers, and board members. Susan spent two hours helping her develop a business plan.

When the check came, she pushed it over to Susan saying, "Well, you sure are more successful than I am right now. So I'll get the next one." Susan paid it, but felt abused. What she should have said with a wise smile was, "My dear, there is no free lunch. I think this is yours."

Leaving with Grace

If you are with someone who is thoroughly enjoying themselves and doesn't seem to want to wind things up, then ask for the check, pay it, put your napkin on the table, and scoot the chair back a bit. If your meal mate's body language doesn't reflect yours, you may need to address the departure verbally and say, "It was such a pleasure having lunch (or dinner) with you and I am looking forward to doing it again." You are under no obligation to indicate you have another pressing matter or another client waiting for you in your office.

> Busy people in business realize that a lunch or breakfast doesn't extend past one and a half to two hours. Dinner should wind up after two and a half to three hours.

Graciously end the meal and don't go into explanations. Busy people in business realize that a lunch or breakfast doesn't extend past one and a half to two hours. Dinner should wind up after two and a half to three hours.

No Conspicuous Consumption— Except When It's Necessary

If a business meal is for relationship building, or celebrating with clients because you have closed a big deal, don't go to the priciest restaurant and order the most expensive wine or champagne. You will look as though you are trying to bribe the client, that you charge too much money for your product, or that you don't have much loyalty to your company. Conspicuous consumption went out with the 1980s.

However, in metropolitan areas and when crowds and parking will be difficult, consider going to the expense of hiring a car for the evening. Although it may sound like a luxury, a limousine will allow you and your guests to arrive safe, dry (if it is raining), and on time.

The junior person or host always takes the jump seat or whatever is left after everyone else has gotten in. Car service fees are generally charged to credit cards with a 15 to 20 percent tip added.

Tips for a Cocktail/Networking Party

- Don't overload your plate. Pick out your favorite items and then just nibble. If you are extremely hungry, find an out-of-the-way seat, eat, and then resume mingling. Don't complain about the food, the drinks, or the décor. Stay away from foods that are hard to eat or sticky like honeyed chicken wings or anything with a messy sauce. Select foods eaten with toothpicks.
- If you are standing up, don't try to eat and drink at the same time.
- Hold your beverage in your left hand so that your right hand will not be wet, cold, and clammy to shake.
- If you are talking to someone who is constantly scanning the room, move on to someone else.
- Don't spend more than five or ten minutes with anyone. The idea of a cocktail party is to mix and mingle. You can always excuse yourself to get a drink or go to the restroom.
- It is easier to attend a networking session if you go with someone you know. Just don't stay with that person all night. Otherwise, you have defeated the purpose of the event.
- Be respectful of personal space. Don't stand closer than three feet to someone else unless the room is very crowded. Everyone likes to maintain their bubble of personal space.
- When meeting a celebrity or highly placed executive, take the initiative to greet them. Often a cocktail event is the only time we have access to high-ranking people. But don't overstay your welcome. Introduce yourself, say a few words, and then move on. Don't monopolize his or her time.

It's Not Lemonade, It's the Fingerbowl

Table manners are mostly a matter of practice, common sense, and aesthetics. But here are some that may not be so apparent:

- The napkin goes on the lap as soon as everyone is seated. Never tuck it into the waistband or anchor it on a button.
- A formal table setting will give the diner an introduction to what will be served. A cocktail fork, a soup spoon, a flat, notched fish knife, and a dessert fork all foretell things to come.
- When presented with a formal table setting, always start from the outside utensils and work to the inside.
- In deciding what salad belongs to you and which roll to eat, remember the acronym SLLRP. Solids to the left. Liquids to the right, please. You will always find your butter plate and salad to the left of your plate. Liquids like coffee, tea, wine, and cocktails are on the right. If you have ever eaten at a crowded table, you know how easy it is to eat someone else's roll or drink from the wrong water glass.
- If you are not drinking wine, don't turn over the glass. Wine glasses are routinely picked up if they are not used. But the only glass that is removed during the meal is the sherry glass.
- Crisp bacon, asparagus, artichokes, olives, hors d'oeuvres, and crudités (raw vegetables) are properly eaten with the fingers.
- Shrimp cocktail is not cut into smaller pieces. Spear each piece with the cocktail fork and nibble.
- Bread is rarely served at a formal dinner, partly because there is already so much food and you don't want to fill up on bread. But if it is served and there is no bread and butter plate, then it is permissible to place the roll on the tablecloth. The term "breaking bread" should be taken literally. The knife is reserved for buttering the bread, not sawing the roll in half. Break off only a bite-sized piece of bread or roll, then butter it and eat.
- Food should be passed counterclockwise. Salt and pepper are passed together.
- Never do more than gently wipe your nose in public. Anything more enthusiastic should be done alone.

- It is perfectly acceptable to eat the garnish on your plate.
- Your role as the host or hostess is to anticipate the needs of your guests. If they order iced tea or coffee, make sure to pass the sugar and cream. Pay attention when they place their order. Some people are too shy to send back food that isn't prepared properly or ask for something that was not delivered to them. You will always be remembered for your graciousness and attentiveness.

Relationship Building

Taking the time to cultivate business relationships through the breaking of bread will build bonds. When we connect on a more personal basis and let others know that we value them enough to spend extra time with them, trust is created and business gets completed.

sixteen

16

Participating in Business Events:
Parties, Corporate Outings,
and Gift Giving

*The more guests you have, the more brilliant. The fewer you
have, the more enjoyable will the occasion be.*

—*Manners, Culture and Dress, 1890*

Command performances in the business world include the office party, client cocktail parties, the company picnic, social invitations from your boss, the hospitality suite at the sales meeting, the company holiday party, and any organized sports event, cultural event, honorary dinner, or invitation to The Club.

The dichotomy that corporate events present is that they are specifically planned to break down barriers and loosen up behavior. Yet everyone there is being scrutinized to see how well they behave.

A major corporate function is the perfect time to ruin your career in one fell swoop. It's also a perfect opportunity to get to know customers and colleagues in a different light and enhance relationships. Everyone who has control over your career and your advancement will be in attendance.

The dichotomy that corporate events present is that they are specifically planned to break down barriers and loosen up behavior. Yet everyone there is being scrutinized to see how well they behave.

211

Some love the limelight and the social opportunity, others have a strong urge to stay home.

We've borrowed a technique that a late-night television host uses—the Top Ten List. This list, however, has to do with top ten major mistakes that an unsuspecting individual can make at a corporate function. All we need to do is go to one business affair to see nearly every one of these at work.

10. Not showing up

The first rule of business functions is that you can't ignore them. Showing up is important to enhancing presence. Business social events are a perfect opportunity to get to know clients, colleagues, and executives on a more personal level. Leaving early is an option, but respectful entrances occur no later than 15 minutes after the expressed time on the invitation. The old rules of being "fashionably late" have expired. The host or hostess may have planned the evening around a theme or hired special entertainment that it would be inappropriate to miss. Showing up late can also be perceived as being "antisocial" or "too good" to mingle with customers and colleagues.

> 75% of people attending a corporate event are feeling some level of anxiety.

Aside from showing up, it is recommended that you attend the company-sponsored hospitality for at least an hour. Participating in games, dancing, roasting of the president, or whatever else the social committee has thought up is a demonstration of good sportsmanship.

Refrain from staying glued to good friends and familiar colleagues all night. The whole reason for the event is to mix and mingle with new colleagues and higher-ups with whom you generally have limited contact. But the irony is that the empty seat at dinner is usually next to the president. Most people's comfort zone is with peers, not superiors.

9. Ignoring the boss, president, or chairperson because you are afraid of making a faux pas

Employees who ignore their boss at a corporate function are rarely rewarded, promoted, or otherwise recognized. It is like being invited to a birthday party and ignoring the birthday boy or girl; don't expect an invitation for next year. But the more socially inept your boss is, the more gratitude will be felt if you come to the rescue on social occasions.

So why not stretch a little, show some power and presence, and possibly further your career? At minimum, greet the most senior people at a corporate affair and spend three or four minutes talking with each one. Appropriate topics of conversation are the generosity of the company for hosting the event, the festive food and ambiance, light topics of business, and any known hobbies of the host or hostess.

One thing we have all found out about small talk—the more we do it, the easier it gets. The fact is most senior people feel just as awkward and uncomfortable as you do, and probably moreso because they are expected to be smooth and charming.

8. Believing that "business casual" means jeans and a T-shirt

Dressing for the occasion is important to your sense of power and self-confidence. If the affair is formal, be certain that you show up in a tuxedo, not a suit, unless the invitation indicates otherwise. If you attend two or more social events annually that require a tuxedo, plan to purchase one. It is more cost effective, it will fit better, and it is always available.

As a female employee or a male employee bringing a date, find out whether the skirt length will be short or long. Black is always a safe color and velvet, silk, satin, and sequins are wonderful for evening events. Just don't wear anything too sexy, too tight, or too revealing.

If you can't afford to buy something lovely, look in the yellow pages for stores that rent formal wear. Nearly all of them rent dresses and gowns, too.

> True conversation cannot be preprinted. One must bring ready-made ingredients, such as information, experience, anecdotes, and opinions, prepared to have them challenged and to contribute to a new group effort. That is what conversation is: developing and playing with ideas by juxtaposing the accumulated conclusions of two or more people and then improvising on them.
> —Judith Martin, *Miss Manners' Guide to Excruciatingly Correct Behavior*

On the other end of the spectrum is "business casual," one of the most misunderstood and misinterpreted terms in business vernacular. It isn't what you would wear to hang around the house watching football or horsing around with the kids on Sunday afternoon. It doesn't include cutoffs, T-shirts, tank tops, blue jeans, shorts, warm-up suits, or thongs.

> 90% of all U.S. companies allow business casual attire either daily or weekly.
> —ASTD Survey Report

Business casual means well-coordinated outfits. Formality depends on the occasion and the location. Khakis, a well-pressed sport shirt, and deck shoes might be appropriate for a casual dinner after an off-site meeting with your team. Substitute wool trousers for the khakis and leather loafers for the boat shoes and the outfit escalates to the next level. Add a tie and a sport coat and you are prepared for a dressier business casual event such as dinner in a nice restaurant or a cocktail party at a country club. Shorts are not appropriate for daytime meetings, but can certainly work for a luau on the beach.

For women, well-tailored trousers with coordinating blouses, sweaters, or jackets define business casual. Long, straight skirts with a blouse, a turtleneck top, or a sweater set will look polished and professional for daytime sessions. Earrings, scarves, and shoes should be as well coordinated as with any business suit. Summer dresses are a better choice than shorts for events that will take you outside.

7. Gossiping about your boss or colleagues

When you are away from home or in a small group in a smoky bar, it seems the perfect time to let down your guard and express how you really feel about the person you work for. This is a big mistake. No one has a perfect boss. They don't exist. Why point out his or her frailties? When everyone else is spilling the beans on the boss, it is almost irresistible not to add your two cents about how she regularly loses her temper or how he has a drinking problem.

We've all been in the situation of having to confirm rumors such as, "Did you hear he got passed over for the vice presidency because he's overweight?" or "I heard she's having an affair with one of her salespeople." Loyalty is always rewarded. So is having the presence not to give credence to any rumor, true or not, about your boss or a colleague.

It is interesting that topics of conversation that would never be broached in the office become lively talk at an offsite sales meeting. Illustrating a powerful presence may simply mean that you stretch, yawn, and excuse yourself. Even better, dispel the rumor with facts you may know.

6. Overeating and overdrinking

When you significantly overeat or overdrink at a company function, it appears rather low class, as if you rarely get out. One of our seminar attendees sheepishly told us that he got the nickname of "Goober" because he ate so ravenously and even took doggie bags with him at company events.

> You can never go wrong if you are circumspect on your personal bias and generous in your praise.

Early in her career, an associate embarrassed herself by eating so much that when she stood up, her belt popped open and fell off in a loud clatter. As she bent over to pick it up she burped loudly. At that point, she wanted to stay bent over and crawl under the table.

If you love to eat and have a huge appetite, enjoy a large snack before going to an event where you will be dining with business colleagues and clients (Scarlett O'Hara did it). Consider eating after the event is over, and think twice about bringing anything home.

5. Cheating in sporting events

It is very hard to have presence when you are playing a sport with a cheater. It is also extremely difficult to be fully aware of cheating and not be able to do much about it. One of our clients always receives a request to play tennis with the president's wife at the company picnic. If the boss's wife is losing, she frequently calls her opponent's shots "out" when they are not even a close call. Our client decided that it wasn't worth debating over, but she harbors resentment about playing with her.

Professional presence prescribes that you use a great deal of façade and composure when your boss or a customer shaves a stroke off a hole or two during a round of golf. While you may have a strong desire to jump up and down and shout, "Why you cheater! You know it took you seven strokes on that par three," your silence and composure will speak more loudly than words about the depth of your character. You walk away with your dignity intact, your honesty unflawed, and your job secure. Yet you have also been given an important clue: The way someone plays on the sports field is often how they play in the boardroom.

Good sportsmanship is allegorical to business. In fact, chess was created by war-weary leaders so that kings could fight their battles on the chessboard, not the battlefield. The same qualities that are admired in sports are equally admired in business: strategy, persistence, strength, a desire to win, and a sense of fair play.

Here are some good rules for any sport:

- Be perfectly honest about your ability in the sport.
- Be not only on time, but early and ready to play, with the right equipment and the correct attire.
- Never get angry at the poor performance of your opponent or yourself. Abstain from using obscenities.
- Take the intensity level from your host. If this is just a relaxing game of golf designed to build camaraderie, don't play as though you are in the finals at the Masters. On the other hand, don't be a goof-off on the tennis court if you are playing with a serious player.

4. Making a pass at another company employee

Company picnics, quarterly beer parties, and impromptu office celebrations give us the opportunity to look at each other in a different light. Away from the pale fluorescence of an office cubicle, we can get an entirely different perspective of a colleague. Or at least in a smiling, happy atmosphere, the rules seem to get fuzzy.

One of our male clients was flabbergasted when an administrative assistant who had enjoyed one beer too many walked up behind him and grabbed his derrière. She looked at him and said, "You know, I have just always wanted to do that." And then she walked away.

A public or private pass can border on sexual harassment. Don't encourage one and certainly don't make one. You will lose power, respect, credibility, and you could potentially set yourself up for a lawsuit.

3. Losing your composure with a celebrity

Large companies often sponsor parties during industry conventions. These events generally hinge around well-known stars. Nationally recognized personalities like football players, coaches, television news people, best-selling authors, or motivational speakers are frequently invited to make a presentation at huge dinner meetings.

It is a wonderful feeling to have people wildly applaud and show enthusiasm. But we've watched with a mixture of amusement and embarrassment as two mature company employees clung onto the lead singer of a music group after the performance. They figured that since their company had sponsored the event, they were entitled to some extra attention. We have also witnessed full-grown men fall off the stage trying to shake hands and slap the back of an NFL coach.

Don't lose your cool around celebrities. Walk up, shake hands, comment on their stellar performance, and then make way for someone else.

2. Missing your boss's big moment

Most meetings require the participation of at least a score of in-house executives. Some are adept at public speaking and others fairly faint at the thought.

Stay close and very loyal to your boss before, during, and after the big moment. Plan to go to bed early the night before the scheduled speech. Don't even think about closing down the bar that evening. Be energized, helpful, and completely supportive. Pass out handout material, shepherd people into the room, clap loudly, and generally carry on like Ed McMahon. Your boss will love you for it!

Be ready to step in if necessary. A vice president of a computer company had to pinch-hit at the last minute because the president and CEO was literally getting sick in the men's room 10 minutes prior to his address to the industry council. The V.P. stepped in and eloquently took over. To this day, the president is still grateful to his loyal vice president for saving the evening.

1. Believing that you can make a fool of yourself and everyone will forgive and forget

Don't think that what you do at an off-site meeting will not get back to the office and possibly your home. The problem with walking on the wild side at a business function is that you can't win. Casting yourself as a fool, flake, or drunk totally misses the reason for being at the affair.

Don't go to the hotel room of someone of the opposite sex, unless a whole group is going. Don't go out barhopping with the gang, unless you are certain things will stay under control. You will never be faulted for being circumspect, but you could end up in jail if you are party to anything rowdy or illegal.

Don't allow peer pressure to engage you in an activity that you know will somehow damage your reputation. One of our former colleagues went skinny-dipping with five other colleagues of the opposite sex, and forevermore they were referred to as the "Navy Seals." This, of course, required an explanation every time it was mentioned in front of someone not privy to their escapades.

Maintain Your Modesty

One of the most difficult parties to maintain modesty through is the pool party. Company executives and colleagues may throw a pool party as a gesture to put everyone at ease and provide a more relaxed environment to establish camaraderie.

But for female employees, let's look at the reality. First, if you have a well-exercised body with no additional fat or cellulite anywhere, everyone will stare in adoration or lust. Remarks will be made and you may feel victimized. That group of women comprises about .0005 percent of the population.

The rest who are not centerfolds will be forced to display our half-naked bodies before every man in the office, who previously had only seen the flesh on our face, our hands, and 15 inches or so of our leg. Either way, it's a no-win situation.

For men who are extremely out of shape with a large stomach and thin legs, there will still be the requisite "once over" by the group. Because of social conditioning, most men probably won't feel as scrutinized as women do, but most out-of-shape men will admit to being uncomfortable.

> If you have the option, attend the pool party in a nice summer outfit that will give you a better comfort level in front of your peers.

If you have the option, attend the pool party in a nice summer outfit that will give you a better comfort level in front of your peers. You don't have to get in the pool to enjoy yourself.

If you are attending a meeting at a resort where beach activities are planned, both men and women should shop for the most flattering bathing suit and wear a cover-up to and from the beach.

A Generous Gesture

One of the nicest compliments we've received is when a client or vendor invited us to an important company event. To be included in a "family affair" is a wonderful show of generosity and is quite an honor to the person receiving the invitation.

Looking at it from the company's perspective, why not maximize all the expense, time, effort, and imagination that is required for a major event? You can generate additional goodwill and public relations by inviting an "extended business family." It may be as elaborate a tradition as the annual Christmas party, a friendly event like the company picnic, or a special outing like a sporting event, where the company springs for all the tickets plus buses to the stadium.

Look over your client list and create a slate of your favorite customers. Invite 10 or more. There is no doubt that they will be flattered because this is not an invitation that they would regularly receive. Few firms do this. You are singling them out and showing them that they are more than just business contacts. They are valued friends whom you enjoy not only on a professional basis but on a personal one, too.

Business Entertaining at Home

Who has time to invite clients, bosses, or coworkers to their home? Who has time to clean up the house, plan the menu, shop, arrange for childcare, and then make sure everyone is happy, comfortable, and enjoying themselves at your soiree?

Not many people. That is why entertaining at home is such a uniquely wonderful way to make your customers or colleagues feel like very valued individuals. It is a lost art. Since we haven't done it for so long, or we have never done it at all, it can seem like an overwhelming, forbidding, and anxiety-producing event. Why put ourselves through it?

Yet every time we invite business associates to our apartment, condo, cabin, farm, or house in the suburbs, something positive happens. Everyone lets down the business guard and we get to know each other on very different terms. It is more personal, more relationship-building, and more flattering than any request to dine even at the finest restaurant.

There is something about being invited to someone's home that is unlike any other invitation. A table in a restaurant belongs to whoever is seated there at the time. It is transient and temporary. Someone's home is permanent. It shows their taste, their hobbies or interests, their preferences in books, music, colors, gardening, cooking, and all the other things that give richness and fullness to life. Extending an invitation to clients or colleagues for a home event shows that they feel safe and secure enough to share another part of their life.

> Panache starts well before you arrive at any function, but not because you've hired a limousine. Seasoned partygoers understand why they're attending an event. They've done their homework about the other attendees, and they've determined their goals in attending. Then they go to work on their attitude. Do whatever mental gymnastics it takes to put you in a positive frame of mind. Or stay home; there is no alternative if you want to succeed.
> —Etiquette International

But when is it appropriate? When can you invite a coworker over for dinner? How about a boss? Is it smart to invite customers?

Here are the answers.

Having the Boss to Dinner

Inviting your boss to your home is either intriguing you right now or seems totally out of the question. Let's be honest. If your direct boss is a very refined multimillionaire, and you tend toward a rather eclectic look combining Pier One Imports with garage sale and flea market items, you would probably feel very uncomfortable extending an invitation to your home.

But if you are comfortable that there won't be a huge disparity between your environments, take the initiative, once you have already received an invitation from your boss to his or her home. The admonition here is generally to wait until your boss has already felt comfortable opening another dimension of his or her life to you. Also, adding appropriate coworkers creates more commonality and ease of conversation.

One client reports, "As a boss, I am always very impressed when an employee invites me for dinner; I know they have worried about what to serve, how to serve it, and if it will be fancy enough. I admire their efforts and like getting to know them better on their terms."

A seminar participant expressed an interest in ideas for getting to know his boss better. We suggested that he consider inviting his boss over for a casual barbecue. Of course, we couldn't guarantee that the boss would accept, but the guidelines generally are to ask once and gauge the reaction. If the invitation is put off indefinitely, don't ask again. If you are extended a sincere raincheck, then ask again. If you receive an acceptance, feel honored.

Dinner, Dancing, or Drinks?

There is a big difference between having someone over for dinner and planning a genuine party around a theme. A dinner requires a five- to seven-day verbal invitation. It's more spontaneous and requires much less planning than a party. You will also have the opportunity to get to know someone on a more personal basis over dinner at your house.

If you don't want to commit to a whole evening at your home, invite the boss, customer, or coworker over for hors d'oeuvres and drinks. If it is a client, you will always have something to share and discuss on a nonbusiness level.

Also, inviting someone just for drinks and appetizers won't tie you up cooking and serving. You will be able to concentrate on your guests. It works best around a holiday or prior to a company sponsored event.

Generally if you are single, be judicious in inviting another single businessperson to your home. You don't want it to look like something it isn't.

If you are single, you also have the option of inviting someone else from your office to buffer the situation. If you have been with a client the entire day, it is nice to have the infusion of a new person. It also helps establish your company on a more solid footing because of the exposure to two people from the office.

One client reports, "As a boss, I am always very impressed when an employee invites me for dinner; I know they have worried about what to serve, how to serve it, and if it will be fancy enough. I admire their efforts and like getting to know them better on their terms."

One client, Diane, who recently started working with international businesses, decided to invite two male clients from Brazil along with their spouses. Diane admitted that she was extremely nervous because of the cultural differences. She also didn't speak Portuguese, although they spoke English fairly well.

As Diane began serving the food, one of her clients asked, "Would you like some help?" Thinking how nice it would be to have two more hands, she replied, "Why yes, thank you." With that he looked at his wife and snapped his fingers and said, "Help her."

In amazement, she watched his obedient wife follow her into the kitchen. Since it wasn't in anyone's best interest to try and change Brazilian custom and attitudes that evening, she graciously accepted the help and together they brought food to the table.

When dinner was over, her client looked at Diane and said, "Now, it's time for the men to work." He and the other client proceeded to clear the table, scrape the plates, load the dishwasher, scrub the pots, and completely clear the kitchen counters. Diane and the wives sat down and had a ball watching the men in the kitchen.

Diane is a fun-loving type and she stole away and got her camera. As she started taking pictures, the two clients started hamming it up and mugging for the camera. The wives were feeding Diane verbiage in Portuguese, which included, "Very good job," "Keep it up," and then, "Mop the floor and now clean the oven, too." She had no idea what she was telling them, but she repeated the words loudly and with gusto.

The wives ended up getting the last laugh with their little charade, and this event and the pictures that accompanied it have been passed around both companies. Over five hundred people from each firm know the story. A client dinner at home turned into an event that bonded five people, two large international companies, and added to both companies' legend and lore.

A Little Out of the Ordinary

Here is a list of ideas that may spark your interest in getting together with business associates.

1. Have a wine and cheese party where everyone brings a wine from a different region or country.
2. Try an international theme. Assign each person a dish and a beverage from a different country. If you really want to get creative, ask that the individuals dress in the costume of the country they are representing.
3. Do a Mexican party with a piñata, enchiladas, and mariachi music.
4. Try a Hawaiian party with flower or plastic leis, scooped out pineapples with fruit, and island music in the background.
5. Buy beer, make pizzas, and rent a copy of *Mystic Pizza*.
6. Fondue gets people talking.
7. Try a bingo party with lots of booby prizes.

8. Plan a party around the last episode of a favorite television show. One of our clients had a "Seinfeld" party when the last program was aired. The pictures from that gathering were wonderful and everyone received a framed group picture. This type of party takes little time to organize and it is a quick but lively pick-me-up in the middle of the business week.

A Party They Will Never Forget

A party, as opposed to dinner, requires much more time and preparation. It should be done around a theme that can be either an event, like the Super Bowl, a murder mystery night, or a celebration because a new family room or deck was added to the house.

Easy themes to plan a party around are '50s parties, '20s parties, and toga parties. One colleague has gained such notoriety from her fun parties clients and colleagues want to be sure they are always invited. Sharing such an experience always gives a point of reference during future visits and meetings with those who attended.

Invite people you know will participate and who will enjoy one another's company. Make certain everyone gets introduced to everyone else. It's not a bad idea to appoint a co-host or co-hostess to assist with this. Special touches such as guests' favorite foods, special music, and door prizes or party favors let people know how much they are cared for and valued as both clients and as individuals.

Parties don't have to cost a lot. Time, creativity, and imagination can substitute for money spent. Food does not have to be elaborate; it just has to be abundant. It is much more appealing to have two or three large plates and bowls that are overflowing than a lot of small items that require both a great deal of work and more money.

A Party for All the Right Reasons

Parties happen for all kinds of reasons. One of our advertising clients had spent four months working on obtaining the account for a large, national fast-food chain. Everyone in the entire firm was involved, and the excitement of potentially having this food company as a client electrified the entire office. Many personal and family commitments were put aside, and all energies were focused on this project.

But our client didn't get the contract. It went to another advertising agency.

The office was devastated. They were hurt, angry, and indignant. No one was bouncing back. Other projects were languishing. The president called everyone together and gave them a pep talk, but to no avail. Too much energy had been used up and too much creativity expended without result.

> Parties don't have to cost a lot. Time, creativity, and imagination can substitute for money spent.

The president decided that drastic measures must be taken to turn his office around and get productivity back. He invited his entire office, which he had never done before, to his home. He had a "Competitor's Party," which meant that everyone feasted on fast food from the competing chains of their once-potential client. The decorations were a satirical take-off on the former client's restaurant. He wrote and produced a skit that good-naturedly but pointedly helped define the feelings of frustration that everyone in his office was experiencing.

The party was a great success. What he accomplished could never have been done in a restaurant, hotel, or through prolonged staff meetings. The sentence had been handed down to the firm and the only thing to do was get everyone back on track, feeling positive, optimistic, and empowered again. The party at his home did it.

Pointers for Successful Entertaining at Home

1. Invite your guests to help you prepare or serve the food. People enjoy best what they are involved in. That is why it is often most fun to start with a casual dinner the first time and then work up to something more formal. Casual affairs invite participation. Generally, formal dinners don't allow much except maybe the carving of the meat or the uncorking and pouring of the wine.

2. Break the ice, but don't accomplish that by pushing liquor. Instead, do your homework on each invited guest so that you can have an engaging discussion with everyone, plus give guests conversational information about each other.

3. Do at least one original thing. It can be a stuffed dummy sitting on your front porch dressed up in a business suit with a sign that says "Welcome Mr. Higgins," if your boss or client has a sense of humor. Or it can be one beautiful flower on every person's plate.

4. Don't spend more than you can afford. Don't try to impress business associates with lavish spending. The best parties are those that bring people together emotionally, and that has more to do with chemistry and lively conversation than expensive wine and imported caviar.

5. Don't invite friends the first time you invite your boss to dinner. You don't want to look insecure. Also, you want to be free to focus on your boss, not your friends.

    If you invite your boss to a larger party, make sure that all your friends know beforehand who he or she is so that no one sticks their foot in their mouth.

6. Don't try French cuisine or any other complicated cooking unless you are very proficient at it. Aim for something that you know you cook very well, even if it means grilled hamburgers, baked beans, and chips with dip.

7. Rent or borrow what you don't own. Business dining at home is to build business, not bankrupt you.

8. Start small and work up. Pizza can lead to primavera, and that can lead to seafood fettuccine with lobster thermador. Just don't start out with the lobster.

Corporate Gift Giving

Thoughtful, appropriate gift giving reveals an elegance, a sense of savvy, and a display of good breeding that are very important to business. Selecting the right gift both for clients and employees requires a deeper look into what delights them, what they would truly admire.

A corporate gift may be a funny but tasteful card that reflects a shared sense of humor or a beautifully photographed regional calendar. It doesn't have to be a $75 bottle of cognac. If cost containment is an issue, it is far better and shows a great deal more presence to do something small, personal, and tasteful than to decide you can't afford to do something expensive and just skip the idea entirely.

Defining Your Market

Before you choose a business gift, consider the recipient and determine which type of gift is most appropriate. First, be sure to check your client's company policy and respect their environment. Many companies are not permitted to receive gifts of any kind from clients, customers, or vendors.

Then you must decide whether it is appropriate to make a personal selection or whether large numbers of the same gift for multiple recipients is more suitable. A law firm may take the time to personally select gifts for its top 25 clients. One client may receive a book on hunting, while another receives a signed print from a local artist.

On the other hand, a newspaper may want to send 300 Cross pens with their logo to their advertisers as a holiday gift. A real estate company may need 50 congratulatory fruit baskets for new homeowners.

These two types of gifts differ, and it is obvious to a customer receiving one which category they came from. But this doesn't mean that receiving a nice Cross pen with a corporate logo is not a treat. It just means that you have to decide which type of giving is the most appropriate and will create the greatest amount of presence and power for you and your company.

Receive a present in the spirit in which it is given and with a quiet expression of thanks. Never spoil the intention behind the gift you have received by saying it is of little value or use to you or that you have others just like it. Anything, either verbal or non-verbal, that discounts the generosity of a gift is inconsiderate and hurtful.

Giving to the Individual

The month of December is the most traditional for corporate gifts to individuals. Gift companies are always busiest then. But the surprise and pleasure of receiving an executive planner on Labor Day, a book on bed-and-breakfast inns three months prior to your vacation, or popcorn and two movie tickets on a Friday morning will certainly create a wonderful impact.

When possible, always personalize the gift with the client's initials, a personal inscription, or the author or artist's signature. Be sure to include a well thought out, sincere note card, and mention any personal connection that the gift has to the receiver.

Gifts That Are Welcome

- A nicely matted and framed photograph or featured newspaper article about that person.
- A book that reflects the person's hobby or an avid interest. Beautiful art books, photography books, or unusual cookbooks are always a treasure. Hardcover is preferable, but softcover is fine, too. A great deal is added if the book is autographed by the author. Register with local bookstores so that you can be aware of store-sponsored book signings. If you don't have the time or the opportunity to get the author's autograph, be certain to do your own inscription in the front.
- A brass carriage clock for office or home with an appropriate engraving on the back.
- Lead crystal, silverplate, or porcelain from Tiffany's, Saks, or a quality jeweler.
- Leather goods from Mark Cross, Louis Vuitton, Hartman, or Gucci.
- Brass doorknocker with family name.
- A nice print or photograph that has been signed and numbered. Real estate agents and others who rely on long-term referrals should attach their business card on the back of the framed print.
- A video of a favorite old movie.

- A beautifully photographed calendar.
- Cooking paraphernalia like a pasta maker, coffee grinder, or juicer with the appropriate food to accompany them.
- Fine champagne, spirits, wine, or cognac for an occasion that is congratulatory, but only if you are certain that it is a favorite brand. Be sure to mention that on the enclosure card.
- Two theater tickets to a popular performance along with a limousine to pick them up.
- Two movie tickets and a box of popcorn to a movie that you have recommended to a customer.
- Golf sweater or golf balls from the Masters or a very special golf course.
- Handcrafted, signed glass paperweight.
- An antique of any sort. The recipient will know it is special but will never know how much it costs.
- Chocolate chip cookies or any homemade goody. These have special meaning when the treat is made by a single man and presented to a busy mother.

Quantity, But Still Quality

Just because gifts are ordered in large quantities doesn't mean that the quality and the distinction aren't there. Many family businesses give clients smoked turkeys at Thanksgiving or Christmas, which are a very welcome gift.

One client eagerly anticipates the arrival of two fragrant, fresh fir wreaths from a longtime vendor. For him, it is the harbinger of the holiday season. He doesn't care that the same thing is also sent to two hundred other customers.

If gifts include the company's logo, the quality of the item must be good. In the case of IBM, they not only give quality items; they generally place their logo in a very inconspicuous place. One of my friends still enjoys a

When one of our clients received a very nice selection of roasted nuts and pound cake, the vendor that gave it to her said, "Oh, I've got a trunkful of this stuff. I'm trying to get rid of it. Do you want another one?"

lovely crystal fruit bowl, where "IBM" is lightly etched at the bottom and only visible once the fruit is gone. If IBM had been blasted on the side of the bowl, she probably never would have used it.

Nice, quality gifts

- A basket of food, which can include either fresh items or boxed ones like gourmet crackers, cheese, and preserves. The best baskets have at least one durable item. Many companies will include an item with a company logo.
- Fresh fruit or hors d'oeuvres on handcrafted, one-of-a-kind, signed platters bring both an immediate pleasure and a lasting one.
- One company in Seattle keeps an artist busy supplying them with fruit bowls that feature apples, which are then filled with real apples plus a special card, noting how the artist made the handcrafted bowl. It is a delightful, well thought out corporate gift.
- Regional food that is sent to local clients doesn't have much of an impact. But when smoked salmon is shipped to a customer in Ohio, it is a treat. Other regional treats might include:

  - Salmon from the Northwest;
  - Peaches, peanuts, and grits from the South;
  - Lobsters and clam chowder from New England;
  - Oranges and grapefruit from Florida or California;
  - Steaks from Texas;
  - Cheesecake from New York;
  - Amish cheese from Pennsylvania or Ohio.

- Good quality chocolate candy with or without a corporate logo.
- A subscription for a monthly gourmet fruit or coffee delivery to a customer's home.
- Gourmet popcorn in 5-gallon-sized containers.
- A gift certificate to Franklin Covey or other business resource companies.

- A leather portfolio with the recipient's initials on the outside and your corporate logo in an inconspicuous place on the inside.
- A gold pen with recipient's initials engraved on the side and a company logo, if desired.
- A desk set with the client's initials engraved on a small brass plaque.
- A high-quality letter opener with client's initials and small corporate logo, if desired.

Charitable Gifts

There are other gifts that show presence and a sense of concern for others. Charitable contributions to Meals on Wheels, the Food Bank, the Boys and Girls Club of America, Girl Scouts, the Historical Society, and the YMCA made on behalf of the customer, show a philanthropic concern while honoring your client.

Chicago's major bond underwriting firms decided that rather than host a $150,000 bash to celebrate the successful Chicago city bonds, the money would be better used by the hungry people of Chicago. Each of the bond houses contributed the same amount of money that they would normally have given to the big society event. Invitations were sent asking invitees not to show up for an event that wasn't going to happen due to party-planning funds being redistributed to the needy. It was a gift that demonstrated sensitivity and concern and generated excellent public relations for the firms involved.

Entertaining Gifts

A very successful lawyer and entrepreneur, Ruth Cate, pays a gracious tribute to her field force, who are sales representatives working on commission. She travels to the account executive's city and has dinner with the representative and accompanying spouse or partner. The next night she has dinner with whichever potential client the account executive selects.

She wines and dines them at a fine restaurant and pays him or her avid attention. It may either be a customer who has purchased a great deal of advertising, or a business that poses great potential but which hasn't bought a thing. The special evening is Ruth's gift to her salesperson.

Travel agencies often buy blocks of sporting event tickets for their customers. The way they "gift" out the tickets is to let their best customers know they are entitled to four seats per year and that all they need to do is call and request the day. They don't accompany the client to the event but do enclose a personal note along with the ticket that says, "Thanks for using Universal Travel. We hope you enjoy the game." The drawback is that they don't spend the personal time with their client.

> To maximize relationship development, if you have two tickets to an event, take a client. If you have four tickets, take two clients and another colleague from your office.

Symphony, opera, and ballet tickets are a wonderful gift if a company has a clientele that enjoys such events. Otherwise, they just get chucked into the wastepaper basket. Special tickets to the opening of a new play or movie are a thoughtful gift, too.

Decide whether an entertaining gift has more presence if you accompany the client, or if it is a more gracious gesture just to send the tickets. It always shows a special touch if you can include something permanent like a wool plaid blanket with football tickets or the compact disc of the opera. But intangible gifts are just as powerful, welcome, and thoughtful as tangible ones.

Unexpected Gifts

Sometimes the gift that shows the greatest amount of presence is the one not expected. A company president took the entire office to San Francisco for a five-day meeting; however, spouses weren't included. But on the first day of the meeting, each spouse received a large basket of fruit and flowers. The president personally wrote a note with each that said, although they weren't able to include the spouses, the company wanted to show their appreciation for their support.

Looking a Gift Horse in the Mouth

There are some gifts that are not in good taste or that are simply dated. Wine that is inexpensive or very common is not a good choice. Be very careful you don't give liquor to anyone who is a recovering alcoholic or whose personal convictions or religion forbid it.

Anything that is low-grade plastic, useless, or junky, like key chains or bottle cap openers, is a waste of money. So are plastic pens and inexpensive quartz watches with a company logo on the face. Anything that looks like leftover or obsolete inventory is a disaster. It is better to give this away at the company picnic as booby prizes or find a worthy charity to donate it to.

Global Gift Giving

Although gifts with obvious logos are not always desirable in this country, they are among the most desired of gifts from the United States in nearly all other countries, with the exception of France. Popular gifts that are highly regarded from American hotels to their Pacific Rim customers are wine decanters and glassware with the hotel logo sand-blasted in the center. Crystal globe paperweights with a company's headquarters pinpointed in color are very desirable.

Cross pens with logos, especially if they are internationally recognized company logos, are welcome. Status gifts like fine leather goods with logo imprints are good choices. Logo calendars from American firms are very popular in Europe. For an inexpensive gift, Post-it note pads with the company logo will be used and admired.

Is a Card Appropriate?

Just because someone had a baby doesn't mean you have to send a gift. Just because someone marries doesn't mean you have to find out where they are registered. A gift is never a requirement if you don't attend the occasion.

However, if you attend a boss's, colleague's, or client's invited event, you should bring an appropriate gift. If you are invited but don't attend, then you have the option of a gift or a card. But all-important events, whether you are invited or not, require a card if you want to show consideration and presence.

A pregnancy, a retirement, an adoption, and even a divorce may be the right occasion to let a longtime customer know you are thinking about them. It is nearly impossible to overdo sincere cards of congratulation, celebration, and concern for a person's situation. The death of a loved one is the only time that a purely handwritten note or letter is required.

Keep on hand nice notepaper and a cache of various cards, especially handcrafted cards. These will make it much easier to jot off a quick note.

Gifts in the Inner Office

Some etiquette books will say that it is inappropriate to give your boss a gift. I completely disagree. The gift doesn't have to be expensive, but it is an extremely fine gesture during the holiday season to give your boss a book, a box of favorite chocolates, or an addition to a collection. If it seems more appropriate, you can take up a collection from the staff and purchase a group gift.

For the boss's birthday, unless the year ends in a big "0," a card signed by the entire office is enough.

In large offices, birthdays can get out of hand. Nearly every day is a birthday for someone. Most large companies with big staffs have one party on the first Friday of the month for everyone with a birthday that month. A cake is purchased, balloons are blown up, candles are blown out, the song is sung, and everyone goes back to work.

An important customer's birthday should always warrant at least a phone call, if not a card, lunch, or small gift.

Wrapping and Unwrapping

Great care should be given to the wrapping of the business gift. If the wrapping is poorly done or inexpensive looking, it will directly reflect on the present. If a wrapping service is offered where you purchased the gift, pay a little extra for the luxury wrap.

Try to take the time to present the gift in person. This can be done at a client's office or during a business meal.

The gift should be opened immediately and a verbal thank you, along with well-chosen comments, should be forthcoming. If someone seems confused about whether to open the gift or to wait, graciously suggest that they open it. The exception is with Japanese clients because Japanese manners will not permit them to open a gift in front of the giver.

The Thank-You Note

In the South, there is a time-honored tradition that when a gift is received, a thank-you note should be written before the sun sets that day. This is true of both personal and business gifts. If you don't do it then, you are likely to forget the next day, and so it goes until it seems too late to do anything, and so you do nothing.

Thank-you notes are important. If you don't send one, that will be remembered. If you do, it may not always be remembered, but you won't have a black mark next to your name in the mind of the giver.

The note should be brief and sincere, and it should certainly mention the gift. Don't refer to the item generically, "Thank you so much for the pen." Instead, try, "Thank you so much for the Mont Blanc fountain pen." State your particular fondness for the item and also discuss how you are going to use it.

> Some political observers say that George Bush won the presidency because of thank-you notes. Over his years in public office, he has written literally thousands of personally penned expressions of his gratitude and appreciation to individuals. That kind of thoughtfulness and consideration is rarely forgotten.

A Parting Note

One last word on corporate gifting: Professional presence can never be created solely by giving someone an expensive present. Gift giving can only enhance a business relationship. If even a small gift seems inappropriate, then a simple, sincere, in-person, "Happy Holidays," "Happy Birthday," or "Congratulations on the Baby" is a wonderful, intangible present. Giving doesn't need to necessarily be expensive. It just has to be personal and well thought out.

C

seventeen 17

Including Your Spouse or Partner: An Asset or a Liability?

The utmost care should be taken that all the company will be congenial to one another, and with a similarity of tastes and acquirements, so that there shall be a common ground upon which they may meet.

—*Manners, Culture and Dress, 1890*

A colleague reported that he begged his pregnant wife to accompany him to the annual Christmas party. He felt he just couldn't go to the affair alone. She went, protesting that her dress was ugly and her feet were swollen.

She whined and complained all night to everyone who would listen. The food gave her indigestion, she couldn't drink, her shoes were too tight, the baby was kicking, and why was the band so noisy?

Another associate of ours told us that she invited her new boyfriend to the company picnic. Because she was assigned to coordinate the games, she had to be there early.

He arrived separately, donned a cowboy hat as he emerged from his pickup truck, and walked toward her wearing a tee shirt that said "So many women, so little time." He strode across the field and gave her a loud kiss.

237

Today, many married couples actually prefer to go it alone even when they have the option of bringing a spouse or date.

In both cases, our clients decided they should have gone it alone. Having a spouse or date that doesn't fit in is much worse than being single at a corporate event. Forcing a fit with your partner and your coworkers and clients is a mistake. You will probably feel uncomfortable and compromised.

Today, many married couples actually prefer to go it alone even when they have the option of bringing a spouse or date. It is often easier, more acceptable, and potentially more productive to go sans partner. You then have things fully under your control.

When a Spouse Really Hates Your Office Party

In the case of a spouse or partner who resists exposure to corporate events, even if you dress them up and coach them on what to do and when to do it, the simple fact is, if they don't know the rules of your business world, you will probably end up with three things:

1. An angry and embarrassed partner.
2. Business associates who have seen right through your failed coaching job.
3. An angry you, because it seems that it shouldn't be that difficult for your partner to maintain a professional and appropriate presence for several hours.

If you have a relationship with someone who really dislikes your business and your colleagues, your presence will not be enhanced by dragging them to a company-sponsored event. If they are outwardly hostile or just clam up at such events, vow to keep your personal and professional lives totally separate. Thousands of businesspeople do so and they thrive.

Allowing your spouse his or her own freedom of expression without apology from you shows a great deal of confidence on your part. One of our female clients just shrugs when she is asked why she never brings her spouse, who holds philosophical and political positions that are very different from her firm's, to company-sponsored events. "I care about him so much that I don't want to force-fit him into my world," she replies.

If your attempts at "Pygmalion" don't work out, enjoy future events solo.

Inappropriate Comments

We have seen spouses do the strangest things at business affairs. One spouse walked up to the president's wife and said, "I am sure I know your name, but I just can't remember it. What is it again?" The president's wife repeated her name graciously but was quite stunned.

One husband at the company picnic actively lobbied his wife's boss for a raise. "Laurie isn't very assertive about asking for a raise, but you know and I know that she deserves one."

Spouses and partners, however, cannot be expected to be mechanical robots that you can program to say the right thing to the right person at the right time. But it is in everyone's interest to do some briefing about the people at the event, giving a rundown of all the names and relationships of the top officers and the topics of conversation to avoid.

At a patio party, one of the spouses said loudly, "I'm glad they fired Fred. He was driving the whole office crazy and my wife complained every night about him." The problem was that Fred had not been fired. In fact, he was standing about four feet away!

Pillow talk is a wonderful release. Venting anger and frustration to a loved one is healthy. But those discussions play best in the bedroom, and a partner should know the difference between the irrational rantings of a stressed-out companion and what are legitimate, rational facts; however, both should be considered confidential.

> Venting anger and frustration to a loved one is healthy. But those discussions play best in the bedroom, and a partner should know the difference between the irrational rantings of a stressed-out companion and what are legitimate, rational facts; however, both should be considered confidential.

A spouse joined a group with her husband's boss and two customers, laughing and joking as they all got to know one another. The spouse then turned to her husband's boss and said, "You know, Tom swears at you in the shower every morning, and I mean every morning!" Even though this was meant to be funny and outrageous, Tom's boss did not forget the remark.

Blinded by the Light of Love

We are often blinded by our affections for a spouse or partner. A bright, well-positioned saleswoman brought her boyfriend of six months to a dinner party in a colleague's home. The boyfriend was uncomfortable, so he drank too much and then sat down at the piano. After a few notes he proclaimed loudly to the group, "This is a fine piece of furniture, but as a piano it stinks."

On Monday, she called to thank her colleague for a lovely time and asked, "What did you think of Kirk? Isn't he wonderful!" Her colleague was grateful she wasn't being asked the question in person or the grimace on her face would have made her answer apparent. The saleswoman's affection for her boyfriend did not allow her to see him as an immature individual who didn't have the experience or background truly to be a business asset to this competent and charming woman.

It was not her colleague's place to tell her what she really thought. But she never saw him again with her at business affairs, so someone obviously gave her the word.

Testing the Waters

A good way to see if your spouse or partner is being well received is by the tone of voice and the facial expressions of your business associates when they ask about your partner. If they ask in a perfunctory manner and then look bored with your answer as they change the subject, they are either neutral or negative.

But if they bring up some clever thing your partner said or if they ask about a special project that was mentioned at dinner, you can probably assume that you can continue to include your partner.

The Right Occasions

The climate changes when a spouse is present in a business situation. Even if the spouse is charming and conversant, the other business associates will feel uncomfortable about excluding them when straight business is being discussed. Often, pure business matters are sidestepped because of the confidentiality factor.

> The trend today is not to include spouses at sales meetings, dinner meetings, and corporate retreats.

The only time to bring a partner to a business event is if everyone else will be doing the same thing. If you are the only one to bring your wife or husband to a client dinner, you will put a huge strain on the whole affair.

The trend today is not to include spouses at sales meetings, dinner meetings, and corporate retreats. Most employees of the company are actually relieved because they don't have the pressure of making sure their spouse is happy, introduced, and involved. And companies save a great deal of money.

Also, with so many two-income families, spouses are often wining and dining on their own. One client told us that she and her husband schedule client dinners on the same night so that they can do business independently and have the rest of the evenings in the week to be together.

When Your Spouse Can Help You

We have a dear friend whose husband is European. When she has dinner meetings with new clients from Germany, Switzerland, France, or Italy, she brings Walter along. There is an instant rapport and an immediate bond. The clients have a lot in common with Walter and a sense of shared viewpoint. Her global business always progresses better when she brings her husband.

Another colleague told us that she brings her artist husband to industry functions to ask the questions that she wouldn't dare ask. He can ask the most confidential business questions and not even wince because he is not in the business world.

She is always amazed what he finds out for her by the end of the night. At one convention, through his nonchalant, casual manner, she found out the gross annual billings of nearly all her competitors!

If your partner does fit in, play it to the hilt. If your spouse or partner naturally complements your presence, showcase, include when appropriate, and value him or her. Create opportunities for him or her to be with clients and associates. It will reflect well on you. This is a powerful asset that not everyone has.

Being Single in a Couple's World

Most of us will spend either a few years or our entire career single in a married corporate world. It doesn't pose the problems that it did in the 1950s when wives and husbands were glued together, and unless there was a "real problem," men and women were married by the time they were 22.

Single people should not be treated as outcasts or worse, as a threat to a married person. Individuals whose spouse cannot attend an event due to illness or prior commitment should not feel out of place. Professional presence means helping make everyone feel comfortable and included. Care and consideration to others should be taken when planning or attending a company event.

> Professional presence means helping make everyone feel comfortable and included. Care and consideration to others should be taken when planning or attending a company event.

One single colleague was asked during a staff meeting if she would be bringing a date to the annual holiday dinner. In front of everyone, the assistant said, "The restaurant needs a final count. They will cut us a special deal if we have twenty-four people, but if you don't bring anyone, that only makes twenty-three and we will have to order off the menu." Our colleague looked her squarely in the eye and said, "I will be attending the dinner with my colleagues, so tell the restaurant our final count is twenty-three and we will be happy to order off the regular menu."

We cannot be aware of the details of everyone's personal life, but sensitivity is important when stepping beyond the professional relationship onto personal ground. If you are unsure of someone's situation, ask the person in private and keep the information you learn confidential. Better yet, if there is an issue, ask the individual if there is anything you can do to make the upcoming event easier for them. If someone is recently divorced and the person feels uncomfortable attending alone, arrange for a group of you to go to the event together. If a spouse or partner is ill, arrange a time during the evening for a group of you to step away from the party and phone the person to say he or she is in everyone's thoughts.

> Part of being a true professional is being gracious enough to put others at ease and not making an issue out of their personal situation.

Part of being a true professional is being gracious enough to put others at ease and not making an issue out of their personal situation.

One single friend is in a business that sponsors a lot of formal affairs. She doesn't like to bring a date because she would rather devote her full time to talking to clients and potential clients. She told me that her method was to show up, act like the hostess, and have a wonderful time. She always leaves after the first big group leaves; otherwise she says she would feel it appears she has nothing better to do or that she is just hanging around waiting to be picked up.

She also spends as much time as possible with the wives, both the ones who work at home and those who work outside the home. She makes certain that she shows avid interest in them whether they are discussing a child's bedtime or municipal bonds.

Most spouses are flattered and delighted that she genuinely enjoys talking with them because they often know few other people. She also makes a point of introducing her new friends to each other once she sees a connection between them.

Her clients are thrilled because their spouses thoroughly enjoy themselves and feel connected to the event. She enjoys it because she often hears insightful, personal information about her clients. And it also serves to dispel any potential concern the wives may have because she frequently travels with their husbands. Her manner is so straightforward, direct, and friendly that her gender is not an issue.

The Romantic Getaway— A Horror Story for a Single Person

It can prove to be uncomfortable for single employees when a company president decides to host employees and spouses at the annual sales meeting. Some companies include the "spouse or partner," but it isn't always comfortable to bring someone just for the sake of doing so. Moonlight beach parties, riding two to a moped, and dining in fancy restaurants near the sea is hard to do solo. Married couples sometimes look at this as a wonderful opportunity for their "second honeymoon." This means that singles feel as if they are really intruding when they hook up with a couple.

Is it okay to forego an extended business "couples" trip? If everything looks as though it will be a disaster, and there won't be any other single people, then do a thoughtful analysis. If you decide that your reputation with your boss will stay intact and that four days and nights of singleness will make you feel self-conscious, obvious, and miserable, then decline.

Another option is to devise a plan for modifying the circumstances to work for you. Stay just part of the time and spend the rest in a location of your choosing. Or organize a few group events where everyone is included and bring a number of wonderful books to read and enjoy the break.

Finding a Method That Works for You

We can't always be expected to be the round peg in the round hole. Sometimes a plan is necessary if your circumstances are unusual.

One client has a boss whom she describes this way: "She is single, doesn't flirt, works hard, and knows how to have a good time. I think that she was able to get over some of the rough spots about being single at corporate events because we all knew she had a boyfriend 'back home.' He never showed up and she rarely discussed him, but the fact that we knew he existed kept the lechers away and generally added to her independent style."

Another male client, who is fairly young and single, has learned to create a scenario that allows him to function well at corporate affairs. He asks a married couple that he knows if he can drive with them to the event. He likes to have someone with whom to get the juices flowing. They discuss what the event will entail en route, and he has someone to walk in with.

He uses his married colleagues as his comfort zone when he starts to feel a little insecure. Also, because they generally know more people, they introduce him. He never dreads going single to events because his foolproof system makes him feel valued, confident, and assured.

Dos and Don'ts for Mixing Spouses with Company Events

1. Don't coax an unwilling spouse to an office function. An obviously resentful attitude on the part of your spouse will reflect badly on you, too.
2. Don't be afraid to go to any corporate event without a partner. You will not lose your power or presence if you maintain an attitude of self-confidence coupled with friendliness.
3. Don't invite a new date to a company event if you are single. Wait until you are comfortable with how they will represent themselves to your office. Fair or not, a date's behavior will reflect on you.
4. Do give your spouse background information on the people who will be attending a company event. Also, cover issues that should not be discussed.
5. Do introduce your spouse to at least two people and make sure there is conversation going before leaving to join another group.
6. Don't flirt with anyone at the office in front of your spouse. Don't hug anyone of the opposite sex, even if it is completely innocent. Don't create suspicion and complicate your homelife.

7. Don't stay at your mate's or date's side the entire evening. This is an important time for both of you to mix and mingle.

8. Don't ever criticize your partner in front of the boss or your colleagues.

9. Do laugh at your spouse's or partner's stories, even if you are the only one laughing.

10. Do make your partner look smart, capable, and valued in front of others.

Conclusion and Action Plan

Professional presence, with all the extraordinary opportunities it presents to us, will expand our horizons. It will give us the support, confidence, and expertise to venture with assurance into business situations that may previously have appeared intimidating.

Having presence will not guarantee any of us a smooth ride free of obstacles. We will never hold all the cards in the proverbial card game. There is an old Chinese proverb that states, "The gem cannot be polished without friction, nor man perfected without trials." However, incorporating our own well-developed style of presence will significantly increase the odds that we can confidently handle ourselves well, no matter what the situation.

There are three important things to keep in mind about professional presence:

1. *It is personal.* It's okay to project personal style. People want to do business with people they like, people they connect with, and people they trust. Integrate the components of professional presence into your personal style. Adapt the practices that work for you.
2. *It is situational.* This book is comprised of real-life examples from businesspeople across the nation. Solutions, responses, and behaviors are situational. What works for one salesperson in one company in one geographic region may backfire in another. What one manager deems to be good leadership skills may not be appropriate for the leadership style of someone else. Your good judgement prevails. So does the context of the situation and the corporate climate. If you are unsure, ask for advice and seek good-quality coaching and mentoring. We can't have all the answers. The issues are too vast; the possibilities, ramifications, and consequences are endless.
3. *Achieving and acquiring professional presence is a lifelong process.* We have to be open to feedback and to continuous learning. Today's fast pace of business puts us into new situations every day, where we have only a brief time to establish a business relationship. We must remain open, aware, conscious, and flexible in each encounter and consistently evaluate what we have learned.

Professional presence will help you gain and maintain control in business. It will provide the resources to enhance, enrich, and empower your entire career.

Review the Professional Presence Quiz in the introduction. You should find that your score is higher after reading the book! Next, complete the following questions. You decide the areas in which you will begin the process of enhancing your professional presence.

Step 1: Recognize the Inherent Power of Your Professional Presence

Chapter 1: *Make First Impressions Lasting Impressions*

🖉 Write three words that describe the way you would like to be perceived in business.

🖉 What can you do to project these descriptors through your behavior?

🖉 How can you enhance the impression you make on others?

Chapter 2: *Developing the Art of Self-Promotion*

🖉 Who are the people who have the most influence on your career?

🖉 What can you do to enhance your relationship with these individuals?

🖉 What can you do to gain visibility within your company?

Chapter 3: *Contemporary Business Behavior*

🖉 Describe a business situation where you felt uncomfortable or ill at ease.

🖉 What would you do differently to handle the situation?

🖉 What can you do to maintain composure in even the most difficult or stressful business situations?

Step 2: Establish Effective Nonverbal Communication

Chapter 4: *The Language of Presence, Posture, Handshakes, and Eye Contact*

✐ List three things you can do to enhance the first impression you create:
1)
2)
3)

✐ What 3 gestures, mannerisms, or behaviors regularly create pitfalls and problems for you? Please describe and then list strategies for overcoming them.
1)
2)
3)

Chapter 5: *Using Space, Territory, and Mirroring and Matching to Make a Connection*

✐ With whom do you have the best rapport and why?

✐ List any coworkers or customers who may have a cultural background different from your own.

✐ What can you do to be respectful of their comfort level with nonverbal communication, such as space and territory and mirroring and matching?

Chapter 6: *Taking Charge Through Nonverbal Communication*

✐ What can you do to become more aware of the way you are perceived as a result of your nonverbal communication?

✐ In what ways can you use nonverbal communication skills to more effectively build connection and rapport with customers and colleagues?

✐ In what ways can you use nonverbal communication to leverage your personal power and presence?

Step 3: Create Your Virtual Presence

Chapter 7: *Electronic Etiquette: Using Both High Tech and High Touch*

✐ If you are not already using technology, how can you incorporate the use of it into your business practices to become more efficient and effective in what you do?

✐ How will you build effective business relationships with those with whom you communicate predominantly through technology?

Chapter 8: *Phone Presence: Office, Cell, Conference, and Voice Mail*

✐ What steps will you take to enhance your telephone presence?

✐ How can you enhance your voice mail presence?

Chapter 9: *The Use and Abuse of E-Mail: How to Get the Best from It*

✐ What steps will you take to enhance your e-mail communication?

✐ What can you do to incorporate "human moments" into your e-mail communication?

Step 4: Understand Business Etiquette

Chapter 10: *Effective Meeting Management*

✐ In what ways can you enhance your presence when leading meetings?

✐ In what ways can you enhance your presence when participating in meetings?

Chapter 11: *Dangling Conversations: Gossip, Grapevine, and Jokes*

✐ What can you do to control gossip and speculation that may be occurring in your office?

Chapter 12: *The Pitfalls, Limitations, and Realities of Office Romance*

✐ What do you consider to be the most important points in this chapter?

✐ Is there any information that is directly related to your workplace?

Chapter 13: *Damage Control: Managing Critical Circumstances and Sticky Situations*

✐ Think of a situation in your office or your company that is in need of "damage control." What can you do to play a role in providing a solution or being part of the solution to move things forward?

✐ Think of a business situation in which you have felt uncomfortable or embarrassed. What did you do or what could you have done to put yourself, a colleague, or customer at ease?

Chapter 14: *Business Travel: Navigating Etiquette on the Road*

✐ What steps can you take to increase your personal comfort when traveling for business?

✐ What can you do to enhance your presence when traveling for business?

✐ What can you do to make your day more productive when traveling for business?

Step 5: Develop Social Savvy

Chapter 15: *Planning the Business Meal: Gracious, Sophisticated Manners*

✐ List three customers, clients, or colleagues with whom you believe your business relationship might be enhanced through entertaining them at a business breakfast, lunch, or dinner.
1)
2)
3)

✐ What can you do to be more comfortable hosting customers, clients, or colleagues at a business meal or networking event?

Chapter 16: *Participating in Business Events: Parties, Corporate Outings, and Gift Giving*

✐ What event can you plan in the next 60 days that would provide enjoyment and connection for you and several of your customers?

✐ Which customers or colleagues might you engage socially to enhance your business relationship?

Chapter 17: *Including Your Spouse or Partner: An Asset or a Liability?*

✐ Are there business events or situations when it is best to attend by yourself?

✐ In what ways can your spouse or partner be an asset to you at business events?

✐ Determine the business events at which you should include your spouse or partner.

Index